PREVENTION MAGAZINE'S
QUICK & HEALTHY LOW-FAT COOKING

Light Ways
with Poultry

Savory, satisfying meals
made with versatile, low-fat chicken,
turkey and game hens

❧ ❧ ❧

Rodale Press, Inc.
Emmaus, Pennsylvania

QUICK AND HEALTHY LOW-FAT COOKING

Managing Editor: JEAN ROGERS
Executive Editor: DEBORA T. YOST
Senior Book Designer: ELIZABETH OTWELL
Art Director: JANE COLBY KNUTILA
Associate Art Director: FAITH HAGUE

Light Ways with Poultry was produced by Rebus, Inc.
Recipe Development: MIRIAM RUBIN
Writer and Recipe Editor: BONNIE J. SLOTNICK
Art Director and Designer: JUDITH HENRY
Production Editor: SUE PAIGE

Photographer: ANGELO CAGGIANO
Nutritional Analyses: HILL NUTRITION ASSOCIATES

Library of Congress Cataloging-in-Publication Data

Light ways with poultry: savory, satisfying meals made with
  versatile, low-fat chicken, turkey and game hens.
    p.   cm. — (Prevention magazine's quick & healthy low-fat
cooking)
  Includes index.
  ISBN 0–87596–277–7 hardcover
  ISBN 0–87596–245–9 paperback
  1. Cookery (Poultry) 2. Low-fat diet—Recipes. 3. Quick and easy
cookery. I. Series.
TX750.L54 1995
641.6'65—dc20   95–8545

Distributed in the book trade by St. Martin's Press

2   4   6   8   10   9   7   5   3   hardcover
2   4   6   8   10   9   7   5   3   1   paperback

CONTENTS

❧ ❧ ❧

PREFACE

ঞ্ঝ   ঞ্ঝ   ঞ্ঝ

Not so long ago, chicken was saved for special occasions, most notably Sunday dinner:
It was just too expensive for the average family to consume more often. Turkey appeared
even less frequently, being reserved for major holidays like Thanksgiving. Again, cost was
a factor, and the sheer size of the bird was another consideration—the hours needed to
roast it and the endless leftovers of which everyone quickly grew tired.

Today, things are different. Poultry is plentiful, affordable and available in a wide
variety of forms, so you can buy as much or as little as your appetite and family size dic-
tate. You can, so to speak, customize your bird, putting an end to squabbles over who
gets the white meat or the drumstick. And you can now choose from a range of indi-
vidual turkey parts to allow for just the amount of leftovers you like—or none at all.

Light Ways with Poultry gives you more than 50 great new ways to enjoy chicken,
turkey and Cornish hens. We've included everything from simple sautéed, baked and
broiled dishes to stir-fries, soups, stews, salads and sandwiches. There's a quick roast
chicken with savory rice dressing and double-onion gravy as accompaniments. There are
Asian, Mexican and all-American versions of poached chicken breasts as well as a
quartet of sauces—low in fat, high in flavor—for perking up plain white meat.

Poultry's versatility is a key to its popularity: These mild-flavored meats marry well
with all sorts of vegetables and fruits. The proof is in our recipes for chicken with
pears, turkey with apples, lemon-rosemary chicken, garlic-lime game hens, chicken-corn
chowder, tropical chicken salad and the like. In fact, the recipes in this book will give you
enough new and exciting ideas for a month of Sundays—without requiring you to rel-
egate chicken and turkey to either Sunday dinners or once-a-year holidays.

Jean Rogers

JEAN ROGERS
Food Editor
Prevention Magazine Health Books

INTRODUCTION

❧ ❧ ❧

What's for dinner? So often these days—and much to everyone's delight—the answer is, "Chicken!" Meals planned around poultry (turkey and game hens as well as chicken) please busy cooks and demanding families. Versatile and inexpensive, poultry boasts a low fat content—a fact that has caught the attention of the health-conscious. Just as an example, a 3-ounce serving of skinless roast turkey breast has 154 calories and less than 1 gram of fat; the same portion of prime rib has 320 calories and 21 grams of fat. While beef consumption has declined substantially since 1980, Americans now eat nearly twice as much chicken (and more than twice as much turkey) as they did in 1970.

New market forms of poultry offer lots of options: You can buy whole chickens and turkeys of various sizes (broilers, fryers, roasters) and whole game hens or halves as well as halved or quartered chickens and turkeys, bone-in and boneless breasts, breast cutlets, steaks or tenderloins, thighs, drumsticks and wings. Remember this tip to keep poultry dishes light: When poaching, stewing, braising or sautéing, remove the skin before cooking; when grilling, broiling, roasting or baking, cook with the skin on (to conserve moistness and flavor) and remove it before eating.

Poultry cold cuts and sausages are often leaner than the beef or pork versions; read the labels, though, for the bottom line. Ground skinless chicken or turkey breast (you can grind it yourself in a food processor) is an excellent substitute for ground beef or pork. For the quickest meals of all, use ready-cooked (roasted, rotisseried, barbecued or smoked) poultry from the supermarket or deli. Remove the skin and slice, dice or shred the meat for sandwiches or salads, or reheat it in the oven or microwave. Preparing a poultry dinner from scratch could hardly be simpler, though.

For a weekday family meal, sauté turkey cutlets with your favorite herbs and serve with green beans and pasta; or stir-fry chicken strips with peppers and snow peas and spoon the mixture over steaming rice. Special-occasion menus can be equally easy: Rub a pair of game hens with a mixture of herbs, spices, lemon juice and olive oil; grill the birds and serve on a platter of quick-cooking couscous.

For convenience— and to avoid last-minute shopping trips—keep some frozen chicken or turkey portions on hand; but for the best flavor, buy poultry fresh for use within a day or two. Because raw poultry is highly perishable and susceptible to contamination by the *salmonella* bacteria (which can cause food poisoning), observe the following precautions: Refrigerate poultry promptly in its original wrappings. Don't allow raw poultry to contact other foods. Wash the cutting board, knife and other utensils—as well as your hands—with hot, soapy water after handling raw poultry. Always cook poultry thoroughly—to an internal temperature of 180° for whole birds, 170° for bone-in parts and turkey breast roasts and 160° for boneless parts. (Or check for doneness be piercing the meat at the thickest point with a sharp knife: the juices should run clear or yellowish, not pinkish.) Thaw frozen poultry in the refrigerator, in a basin of cold water or in the microwave. Do not re-freeze thawed poultry.

Now you're ready to start cooking. Flip through this book and you'll find noteworthy recipes for sautéed, stir-fried, baked and broiled poultry, as well as soothing soups, novel salads and hearty sandwiches. Is your heart set on a traditional chicken dinner with all the fixings? On pages 8 through 15 you'll find a low-fat update of that classic meal, as well as three recipes for flavor-infused poached chicken breasts and four vibrant sauces to serve with poached, baked or broiled poultry.

HOMEMADE CHICKEN STOCK

❧ ❧ ❧

Want a flavorful low-sodium, low-fat chicken stock? Make it yourself. Stock-making takes time, but for two hours the pot bubbles away virtually unattended and you can focus on other projects. You don't even need to peel the vegetables (but do wash them thoroughly). Freeze the stock in 1-cup containers.

> 5 **pounds chicken parts, such as necks, backs, wings and drumsticks**
>
> 6 **quarts water**
>
> 2 **medium onions halved**
>
> 2 **medium carrots, cut up**
>
> 2 **celery stalks with leaves, cut up**
>
> 1 **whole head garlic, cut in half crosswise**
>
> **Small handful of parsley stems**
>
> 4 **bay leaves, preferably imported**
>
> 1 **tablespoon whole black peppercorns**
>
> 1 **teaspoon dried thyme**
>
> 1 **teaspoon salt (optional)**

1 Put the chicken parts in a large colander and rinse under cold running water; drain.

2 Transfer the chicken to a large stockpot and add the water, onions, carrots, celery, garlic and parsley. Cover and bring to a boil over high heat (this will take about 30 minutes). Skim off the foam that rises to the surface, then stir in the bay leaves, peppercorns and thyme.

3 Reduce the heat to low (the liquid should be barely simmering) and cook, uncovered, for 2 hours, skimming the surface as necessary. Remove the pot from the heat.

4 Using a skimmer or slotted spoon, remove as much of the solids from the broth as possible. Place the pot of stock in a sinkful of cold water to cool it quickly, changing the water as necessary.

5 Strain the stock through a fine strainer into a large bowl, and season with the salt, if using. Refrigerate the stock overnight. Skim off the fat that has risen to the surface and store the stock in the freezer for up to 3 months or in the refrigerator for a week.

Per cup 30 calories, 1.2 g. fat, 0.3 g. saturated fat, 0 mg. cholesterol, 46 mg. sodium **Makes 5 quarts**

QUICK ROAST CHICKEN

❧ ❧ ❧

A halved broiler-fryer cooks more quickly than a whole bird and tastes even better than a plain roast chicken if you treat it to an under-the-skin seasoning rub with lemon and herbs. This recipe is enough for dinner for four, with four portions of leftovers.

> 1 **large lemon**
>
> 2 **garlic cloves, minced**
>
> 2 **teaspoons extra-virgin olive oil**
>
> 1 **teaspoon dried thyme, crumbled**
>
> ½ **teaspoon dried rosemary, crushed**
>
> ½ **teaspoon freshly ground black pepper**
>
> ¼ **teaspoon salt**
>
> **One 3-pound broiler-fryer chicken, halved**

1 Preheat the oven to 475°. Set a broiler-pan rack or wire cooling rack in a jelly-roll pan and spray the rack with no-stick spray.

2 Grate enough zest from the lemon to measure about 2½ teaspoons. Squeeze 2 tablespoons juice from the lemon into a cup.

3 Add the lemon zest, garlic, oil, thyme, rosemary, pepper and salt, and mix well.

4 Rinse the chicken and pat it dry. Loosen the skin on the bird by working your hand underneath the skin from the cut side, starting at the breast. Loosen the skin over the thigh as well. Spoon some of the herb mixture under the skin and press down on the skin to spread the mixture evenly, working it into the thigh area. Spoon the remaining herb mixture over both sides of the chicken and place the chicken halves, cut side down, on the prepared rack.

5 Roast the chicken for 30 to 35 minutes, or until the skin is crisp and browned and the juices run clear when the thigh is pierced with a sharp knife. Transfer the chicken to a platter and let stand for 5 minutes for easier carving.

6 Carve one of the chicken halves into serving pieces, reserving the other half for another meal. Remove the skin before eating.

Per serving 177 calories, 7.7 g. fat, 1.9 g. saturated fat, 76 mg. cholesterol, 143 mg. sodium **Serves 8**

Rice and Mushroom Dressing

❧ ❧ ❧

Wild rice and dried mushrooms can be expensive, but a little of each goes a long way in this recipe. The wild rice is combined with brown rice to "stretch" it, and just a half-ounce dried mushrooms produces a deeply flavored broth when steeped in boiling water. You can prepare the dressing in advance through step 6, then refrigerate it in the baking dish. Allow 10 to 15 minutes additional baking time if the dressing has been refrigerated.

¾ cup uncooked brown rice

¼ cup uncooked wild rice, rinsed

1 large shallot, minced

1 bay leaf, preferably imported

1¾ cups cold water

½ cup defatted chicken broth

½ ounce dried mushrooms, such as porcini

1 cup boiling water

½ teaspoon olive oil

2 garlic cloves, minced

¾ teaspoon dried tarragon, crumbled

½ teaspoon dried sage, crumbled

½ teaspoon freshly ground black pepper

⅛ teaspoon salt

8 ounces small fresh mushrooms, quartered

1 tablespoon Port wine or Madeira or additional broth

2 large egg whites

1 In a heavy medium saucepan, combine the brown rice, wild rice, shallots, bay leaf, cold water and ¼ cup of the broth. Bring to a boil over high heat. Reduce the heat to low, cover and simmer for 40 to 45 minutes, or until both the brown rice and the wild rice are tender and the liquid is absorbed. (The wild rice will retain some "bite".) Remove and discard the bay leaf. Remove the pan from the heat and set aside, partially covered.

2 While the rice is cooking, place the dried mushrooms in a medium heatproof bowl and pour the boiling water over them. Let stand for 10 to 15 minutes, or until the mushrooms have softened. Using a slotted spoon, transfer the mushrooms to a plate. Strain the soaking liquid through a cheesecloth-lined strainer set over a small bowl, leaving behind any grit. If the mushrooms are large, chop them coarsely.

3 Preheat the oven to 450°. Spray a shallow 2-quart baking dish with no-stick spray.

4 In a large no-stick skillet, combine the oil, garlic, tarragon, sage, pepper and salt. Sauté over medium heat, stirring constantly, for about 1 minute, or until the garlic and herbs are fragrant. Add the fresh mushrooms and toss to coat well with the garlic mixture. Pour in 2 tablespoons of the remaining broth and the Port or Madeira (or additional broth).

5 Sauté the fresh mushrooms, tossing frequently, for 3 to 4 minutes, or until tender and lightly browned, adding the remaining 2 tablespoons broth, 1 tablespoon at a time. Add the dried mushrooms and their soaking liquid, and simmer for 4 to 5 minutes, or until the liquid is reduced by half. Remove from the heat.

6 Add the rice and the egg whites to the mushroom mixture and stir to blend well.

7 Transfer the rice mixture to the prepared baking dish. Bake for 20 to 25 minutes, or until the top is lightly browned.

Per serving 144 calories, 1.6 g. fat, 0.2 g. saturated fat, 0 mg. cholesterol, 152 mg. sodium **Serves 6**

DOUBLE-ONION GRAVY

✽ ✽ ✽

As tempting as poultry pan drippings might be, you're better off discarding them and making this low-fat gravy from chicken broth. It's useful for saucing potatoes, rice, kasha or leftover turkey. If you like, add a teaspoon of chopped fresh herbs, such as thyme, sage, chives or parsley, to the gravy.

½ teaspoon olive oil

1 medium onion, halved and thinly sliced

½ cup thinly sliced shallots

¼ cup thinly sliced carrots

1 garlic clove, thinly sliced

¼ teaspoon freshly ground black pepper

¼ teaspoon dried thyme, crumbled

¼ teaspoon dried sage, crumbled

1 cup defatted chicken broth

2 tablespoons all-purpose flour

½ cup water

1 teaspoon fresh lemon juice

1 Brush the bottom of a heavy, medium no-stick skillet with the oil and warm it briefly over medium-high heat. Stir in the onions, shallots, carrots, garlic, pepper, thyme and sage. Gradually adding 4 tablespoons of the broth, 1 tablespoon at a time, sauté the vegetables for 5 to 6 minutes, or until the onions and shallots are lightly browned and tender. Reduce the heat, if necessary, to prevent the vegetables from scorching.

2 Place the flour in a medium bowl; slowly whisk in the remaining ¾ cup broth and the water until well blended.

3 Pour the broth mixture into the skillet and bring to a boil, stirring constantly. Reduce the heat to medium-low and simmer, stirring often, for 5 minutes, or until the gravy is thickened and no longer tastes of raw flour.

4 Remove the skillet from the heat and stir in the lemon juice.

Per serving 41 calories, 0.7 g. fat, .05 g. saturated fat, 0 mg. cholesterol, 169 mg. sodium **Serves 6 (makes 1⅔ cups)**

ASIAN POACHED CHICKEN BREASTS

❧ ❧ ❧

You can save the cooking liquid, refrigerate it for up to a week and poach another batch of chicken in it. Bring the liquid to a full boil before reusing it.

¾ **cup defatted chicken broth**

1½ **cups water**

½ **cup sliced scallions**

2 **tablespoons rice vinegar**

2 **tablespoons reduced-sodium soy sauce**

4 **thin slices fresh ginger**

2 **garlic cloves, smashed**

1 **teaspoon dark sesame oil**

¼ **teaspoon crushed red pepper flakes**

1 **pound skinless, boneless chicken breast halves (4)**

1 In a large skillet, combine the chicken broth, water, scallions, vinegar, soy sauce, ginger, garlic, oil and red pepper flakes; cover and bring to a boil over high heat. Reduce the heat to medium and simmer for 5 minutes to blend the flavors.

2 Add the chicken breasts to the poaching liquid and reduce the heat to medium-low; the liquid should be barely simmering. Cover and cook for 5 minutes, then turn the chicken breasts (use tongs so that you do not pierce the chicken) and poach for 5 to 6 minutes longer, or until the chicken is cooked through.

3 Transfer the chicken breasts to plates. Using a slotted spoon, remove the scallions from the poaching liquid and spoon them over the chicken.

Per serving 132 calories, 1.7 g. fat, 0.4 g. saturated fat, 66 mg. cholesterol, 197 mg. sodium **Serves 4**

OLD-FASHIONED POACHED CHICKEN

❧ ❧ ❧

Serve these mildly seasoned chicken breasts with a flavorful sauce, or use them to make chicken salad.

- 1 **cup defatted chicken broth**
- 1 **cup water**
- 1 **small leek, sliced into rings, well washed**
- 1 **small onion, sliced into rings**
- 1 **medium carrot, sliced**
- 2 **tablespoons dry white wine (optional)**
- 1 **garlic clove, crushed through a press**
- ½ **teaspoon freshly ground black pepper**
- ¼ **teaspoon dried thyme**
- ¼ **teaspoon salt**
- ⅛ **teaspoon celery seeds**
- 1 **pound skinless, boneless chicken breast halves (4)**

1 In a large, deep skillet, combine the broth, water, leeks, onions, carrots, wine (if using), garlic, pepper, thyme, salt and celery seeds. Cover and bring to a boil over high heat. Reduce the heat to medium and simmer, stirring several times, for 8 to 10 minutes, or until the vegetables are tender.

2 Add the chicken breasts to the poaching liquid and reduce the heat to medium-low; the liquid should be barely simmering. Cover and cook for 5 minutes, then turn the chicken breasts (use tongs so that you do not pierce the chicken) and poach for 5 to 6 minutes longer, or until the chicken is cooked through.

3 Transfer the chicken breasts to plates. Using a skimmer or slotted spoon, lift the vegetables from the pan and spoon them over the chicken.

Per serving 136 calories, 1.5 g. fat, 0.4 g. saturated fat, 66 mg. cholesterol, 172 mg. sodium **Serves 4**

SOUTH-OF-THE-BORDER POACHED CHICKEN

❧ ❧ ❧

Don't worry about the jalapeño making the chicken super-hot: Diced pickled jalapeños are milder than fresh, and their heat is further diluted by cooking in broth. If you do go for spicy fare, remove the jalapeño bits from the broth after cooking and scatter them over the chicken.

- 1 **cup defatted chicken broth**
- 1¼ **cups water**
- 3 **tablespoons fresh lime juice**
- 2 **garlic cloves, crushed through a press**
- 1 **tablespoon diced pickled jalapeño pepper (optional)**
- 1 **teaspoon ground cumin**
- ½ **teaspoon ground coriander**
- ½ **teaspoon dried oregano**
- ½ **teaspoon freshly ground black pepper**
- **Large pinch ground red pepper**
- 1 **pound skinless, boneless chicken breast halves (4)**

1 In a large, deep skillet, combine the broth, water, lime juice, garlic, jalapeño (if using), cumin, coriander, oregano, black pepper and red pepper. Cover and bring to a boil over high heat. Reduce the heat to medium and simmer the broth for 5 minutes to blend the flavors.

2 Add the chicken breasts to the poaching liquid and reduce the heat to medium-low; the liquid should be barely simmering. Cover and cook for 5 minutes, then turn the chicken breasts (use tongs so that you do not pierce the chicken) and poach for 5 to 6 minutes longer, or until the chicken is cooked through.

Per serving 129 calories, 1.5 g. fat, 0.4 g. saturated fat, 66 mg. cholesterol, 136 mg. sodium **Serves 4**

SALSA CRUDA

❧ ❧ ❧

This classic salsa tastes best at room temperature and should be served soon after you make it. It can be chilled for up to two hours, but if you keep it longer than that the acid in the lime juice will turn the tomatoes to mush. Salsa is virtually fat free, so you can use it lavishly: This recipe yields about a half-cup of salsa per serving—enough to sauce a chicken breast and to leave some salsa on the side for dipping raw vegetables or oven-baked tortilla triangles.

1 pound ripe tomatoes, diced (about 2 cups)

½ cup diced green bell peppers

¼ cup diced red onions

¼ cup chopped fresh cilantro

2 tablespoons fresh lime juice

1 fresh jalapeño pepper, partially seeded and minced (about 1 tablespoon)

½ teaspoon ground cumin

¼ teaspoon salt

¼ teaspoon freshly ground black pepper

1 In a medium bowl, mix the tomatoes, bell peppers, onions, cilantro, lime juice, jalapeño, cumin, salt and black pepper.

Per serving 36 calories, 0.4 g. fat, 0 g. saturated fat, 0 mg. cholesterol, 147 mg. sodium **Serves 4 (makes 2½ cups)**

SWEET-AND-SOUR SAUCE

❧ ❧ ❧

Chinese-style sweet-and-sour sauce is great for dipping grilled chicken kebabs, for basting broiled Cornish hens and for livening up leftover turkey. (It's also good with baked fish.)

¾ cup apricot nectar

3 tablespoons no-sugar-added apricot spread

1¼ teaspoons Dijon mustard

¼ teaspoon ground ginger

3 tablespoons diced red bell pepper

3 tablespoons diagonally sliced scallions

1 tablespoon cornstarch, dissolved in 2 tablespoons fresh lemon juice

1 In a small, heavy saucepan, whisk together the apricot nectar, apricot spread, mustard and ginger. Stir in the bell peppers and scallions, and bring to a boil over high heat. Reduce the heat to medium-low, cover and simmer for 5 minutes to blend the flavors.

2 Stir in the cornstarch mixture and bring to a boil, stirring constantly until thickened.

Per serving 72 calories, 0.1 g. fat, 0 g. saturated fat, 0 mg. cholesterol, 49 mg. sodium **Serves 4 (makes 1⅓ cups)**

HORSERADISH-SOUR CREAM SAUCE

❧ ❧ ❧

This favorite British sauce for beef is also a fine complement for chicken. You can refrigerate any left-over sauce for up to four days.

¼ cup nonfat yogurt

3 tablespoons light sour cream

1 tablespoon snipped fresh chives or thinly sliced scallion greens

2 teaspoons prepared white horseradish

½ teaspoon Worcestershire sauce

¼ teaspoon freshly ground black pepper

⅛ teaspoon salt

1 In a small bowl, using a fork, stir together the yogurt, sour cream, chives or scallions, horseradish, Worcestershire sauce, pepper and salt.

Per serving 60 calories, 2 g. fat, 0.3 g. saturated fat, 0 mg. cholesterol, 203 mg. sodium **Serves 4 (makes ½ cup)**

CREAMY BASIL SAUCE

❧ ❧ ❧

Spread this mixture on poached chicken breasts or use it instead of mayonnaise in chicken salad.

1½ cups loosely packed fresh basil leaves

¼ cup lowfat yogurt

1 tablespoon defatted chicken broth

1 teaspoon extra-virgin olive oil

1 small garlic clove, peeled

2 teaspoons grated Parmesan cheese

⅛ teaspoon freshly ground black pepper

1 In a food processor, process the basil, 2 tablespoons of the yogurt, the broth, oil and garlic until puréed.

2 Scrape the mixture into a small bowl. Stir in the remaining 2 tablespoons yogurt, the Parmesan and pepper.

Per serving 52 calories, 2.3 g. fat, 0.7 g. saturated fat, 2 mg. cholesterol, 77 mg. sodium **Serves 4 (makes ½ cup)**

In the Skillet

✿ ✿ ✿

QUICK, EASY MEALS REPLETE
WITH THE SWEETNESS OF PEARS AND
PLUMS, THE WARMTH OF CURRY,
CHILIES AND GINGER

Chicken Breasts with Pears

½ teaspoon dried thyme, crumbled

¼ teaspoon salt

¼ teaspoon freshly ground black pepper

1 pound skinless, boneless chicken breast halves (4)

2 teaspoons olive oil

½ cup pear nectar

¼ cup defatted chicken broth

2 teaspoons balsamic vinegar

2 teaspoons honey

2 large ripe pears (about 1 pound), cut into ½-inch dice

1 teaspoon cornstarch dissolved in 1 tablespoon defatted chicken broth or cold water

1 teaspoon unsalted butter or margarine

½ ounce toasted coarsely chopped walnuts

The technique used to create this dish is one you can use again and again for quick meals: The chicken breasts are sautéed in a skillet and removed, then a sauce is made in the same skillet, using a few simple ingredients. It's a one-pot meal that can be casual or celebratory, depending on the sauce and side dishes.

1 In a cup, mix the thyme, salt and pepper. Season the chicken on both sides with the herb mixture.

2 In a large, heavy no-stick skillet, warm the oil over medium-high heat. Add the chicken and sauté for 4 to 6 minutes per side, or until cooked through, reducing the heat slightly if necessary. Transfer to a large platter and cover loosely with foil to keep warm.

3 Add the pear nectar, broth, vinegar and honey to the skillet, and bring to a boil over medium-high heat, stirring frequently.

4 Add the pears to the skillet, bring to a boil and reduce the heat to medium-low. Cover and simmer, stirring occasionally, for 2 to 3 minutes, or until the pears are tender. Pour any juices that have collected on the chicken platter into the skillet. Stir in the cornstarch mixture, then the butter or margarine; return the sauce to a boil, stirring gently until slightly thickened. Remove the skillet from the heat.

5 Transfer the chicken to plates; spoon the pears and sauce over the chicken. Sprinkle with the walnuts.

Preparation time 10 minutes • **Total time** 30 minutes • **Per serving** 272 calories, 7.3 g. fat (24% of calories), 1.5 g. saturated fat, 68 mg. cholesterol, 273 mg. sodium, 3.1 g. dietary fiber, 35 mg. calcium, 2 mg. iron, 6 mg. vitamin C, 0 mg. beta-carotene
Serves 4

ON THE MENU
Accompany the chicken with sautéed kale and a mixture of brown and wild rice.

SUBSTITUTION
If pear nectar isn't available, you can substitute apple cider.

FOOD FACT
We owe the development of many modern pear varieties to the French nobility of the 17th, 18th and 19th centuries. Gentlemen cultivated pears as a hobby, and they perfected, among others, the Anjou, Comice and what we now call the Bartlett pear.

Preceding pages: Turkey Sauté with Apples (recipe on page 27)

CHICKEN PICCATA WITH ESCAROLE

12 ounces skinless, boneless chicken breast halves (4)

½ teaspoon dried thyme, crumbled

¼ teaspoon freshly ground black pepper

1½ teaspoons olive oil

2 garlic cloves, minced

5 cups loosely packed cut-up escarole

1 cup halved cherry tomatoes

⅛ teaspoon salt

2 teaspoons cornstarch dissolved in ½ cup defatted chicken broth

½ teaspoon grated lemon zest

1 tablespoon fresh lemon juice

1 teaspoon unsalted butter or margarine

Although it is frequently served as a salad green, escarole is also delicious sautéed with garlic and served warm.

Classic sauces start out rich: Cream, butter and eggs are the basic of many of them. Beyond that, there's a technique called "enrichment," in which more of these luxurious ingredients are added after the sauce is made. Egg yolks and cream may be beaten in, or additional butter whisked into the sauce. Taking a tip from the great chefs, you can also enrich a light sauce like this one; one teaspoon of butter adds just a gram of fat per serving but makes a notable difference in the flavor.

1 Preheat the broiler and a broiler-pan rack.

2 Season both sides of the chicken breasts with the thyme and pepper. Place the chicken on the broiler-pan rack and broil 2 to 3 inches from the heat for about 5 minutes per side, or until it is browned and cooked through. Transfer the chicken to a warm platter and cover it loosely with foil.

3 Meanwhile, in a large, deep skillet, warm the oil over medium-high heat. Add the garlic and sauté, stirring constantly, for 30 seconds, or until fragrant. Add the escarole, increase the heat to high and sauté, tossing frequently, for 2 to 3 minutes, or until the greens begin to wilt. Add the cherry tomatoes and cook for 2 to 3 minutes, or until the tomatoes are warm and soft and the escarole is completely wilted. Add the salt, then transfer the vegetables to the warm platter.

4 In the same skillet, whisk together the cornstarch mixture, lemon zest and lemon juice, and bring to a boil over high heat, stirring constantly. Simmer, stirring, for 1 to 2 minutes, or until the sauce is slightly thickened and bubbly. Add the butter or margarine and any juices that have collected on the platter, and return to a boil, stirring. Cook just until the butter or margarine is melted and the sauce has thickened. Pour the sauce over the chicken and vegetables.

Preparation time 10 minutes • **Total time** 30 minutes • **Per serving** 148 calories, 4.1 g. fat (25% of calories), 1.1 g. saturated fat, 52 mg. cholesterol, 268 mg. sodium, 2.1 g. dietary fiber, 60 mg. calcium, 2 mg. iron, 13 mg. vitamin C, 1 mg. beta-carotene
Serves 4

GOLDEN CHICKEN CURRY

1 cup uncooked converted white rice

2 cups water

½ cup frozen peas

12 ounces skinless, boneless chicken breast halves, cut into ½-inch chunks

3 tablespoons all-purpose flour

1 tablespoon curry powder

¼ teaspoon salt

1 tablespoon olive oil

1 medium onion, chopped

1 large celery stalk, diced

2 garlic cloves, minced

1 cup defatted chicken broth

1 tart medium apple, such as a Macoun, diced

3 tablespoons golden raisins

¾ cup nonfat yogurt

¼ cup chopped fresh cilantro

Fruits go into many Indian dishes: Mangoes, papayas, tamarinds, lemons and limes are used in curries and chutneys. Here, apples and golden raisins give a chicken curry memorable flavor.

1 Combine the rice and water in a medium saucepan and bring to a boil over high heat. Reduce the heat to low, cover and simmer for 20 minutes, or until the rice is tender and the liquid is absorbed. Stir in the peas and remove the pan from the heat; cover and set aside.

2 While the rice is cooking, toss the chicken with 2 tablespoons of the flour, 1 teaspoon of the curry powder and the salt; reserve any excess flour mixture. In a large, heavy skillet, warm 2 teaspoons of the oil over high heat. Add the chicken and stir-fry for 2 to 3 minutes, or until the chicken turns golden (it will not be cooked through). With a slotted spoon, transfer the chicken to a clean plate.

3 Add the remaining 1 teaspoon oil to the skillet. Stir in the onions, celery, garlic, the reserved flour mixture and remaining 2 teaspoons curry powder; sauté, stirring, for 1 minute. Drizzle 2 tablespoons of the broth over the vegetables and reduce the heat to medium. Sauté, gradually adding 2 tablespoons more broth to the skillet, for 3 to 5 minutes, or until the onions are tender and the celery is crisp-tender.

4 Add the apples, raisins and the browned chicken to the skillet, and stir to mix with the vegetables. Add the remaining ¾ cup chicken broth, increase the heat to high and bring to a boil. Reduce the heat to medium-low, cover and simmer, stirring occasionally, for 10 minutes, or until the flavors are blended and the juices slightly thickened.

5 Place the yogurt in a medium bowl. Whisk in the remaining 1 tablespoon flour and the cilantro. Stir a spoonful of the curry sauce into the yogurt mixture; then, stirring constantly, add the yogurt mixture to the skillet. Cook, stirring and shaking the skillet, just until the sauce is heated through. Do not boil. As soon as the sauce is hot, remove the skillet from the heat. Serve the curried chicken mixture over the rice.

Preparation time 15 minutes • **Total time** 45 minutes • **Per serving** 423 calories, 5.6 g. fat (12% of calories), 0.9 g. saturated fat, 50 mg. cholesterol, 508 mg. sodium, 4.1 g. dietary fiber, 161 mg. calcium, 4 mg. iron, 11 mg. vitamin C, 0.1 mg. beta-carotene • **Serves 4**

CHICKEN MOZZARELLA

6 ounces ditalini pasta or other small macaroni

½ teaspoon dried thyme

½ teaspoon dried basil

⅛ teaspoon salt

⅛ teaspoon garlic powder

⅛ teaspoon crushed red pepper flakes

8 ounces thin-sliced chicken breast cutlets, cut into strips

1 teaspoon olive oil

2½ cups halved cherry tomatoes

1 medium zucchini (about 8 ounces), halved lengthwise and thinly sliced

1 cup coarsely diced red onion

¼ cup defatted chicken broth

¼ cup water

1 can (10 ounces) red kidney beans, rinsed and drained

3 ounces shredded part-skim mozzarella cheese

1 tablespoon chopped fresh Italian parsley (optional)

When the word "cheese"—or the name of a specific cheese—is in a recipe title, it's usually a good bet that the dish is loaded with fat. At a restaurant, you'd want to skip anything labeled "Parmigiana," "Mozzarella" or "Con Quattro Formaggi" (with four cheeses). This chicken-and-pasta combination breaks the rule, with less than seven grams of fat per serving.

1 Bring a covered medium pot of water to a boil over high heat. Add the pasta, return to a boil and cook for 5 to 8 minutes, or according to package directions until al dente. Drain in a colander and set aside.

2 While the pasta is cooking, in a cup, crumble together ¼ teaspoon of the thyme and ¼ teaspoon of the basil with the salt, garlic powder and red pepper flakes. Sprinkle the seasonings over both sides of the chicken strips.

3 Brush a large, heavy no-stick skillet with the oil and heat over medium-high heat. Add the chicken strips and sauté for about 2 minutes per side, or until lightly browned and cooked through. Transfer the cooked chicken to a clean plate.

4 Add the tomatoes, zucchini, onions, broth, water and the remaining ¼ teaspoon thyme and ¼ teaspoon basil to the skillet, and toss to blend well. Simmer, tossing frequently, for 4 to 5 minutes, or until the tomatoes have collapsed and the vegetables are tender. Add the beans and simmer for 2 to 3 minutes, or until heated through. Stir in the drained pasta.

5 Place the chicken on top of the pasta and vegetables; pour any chicken juices that have collected on the plate over the chicken and sprinkle with the cheese. Remove from the heat, cover and let stand for 3 to 4 minutes, or until the cheese is melted. Sprinkle with the parsley, if desired.

Preparation time 10 minutes • **Total time** 30 minutes • **Per serving** 375 calories, 6.7 g. fat (16% of calories), 2.6 g. saturated fat, 45 mg. cholesterol, 370 mg. sodium, 5.6 g. dietary fiber, 199 mg. calcium, 4 mg. iron, 23 mg. vitamin C, 0.4 mg. beta-carotene • **Serves 4**

TURKEY SAUTÉ WITH APPLES

3 tablespoons all-purpose flour

1 teaspoon ground cumin

½ teaspoon freshly ground
black pepper

¼ teaspoon salt

⅛ teaspoon ground cinnamon

1 pound thin-sliced turkey breast
cutlets (4)

1 tablespoon olive oil

1 pound apples, cut into
½-inch-thick wedges

¾ cup defatted chicken broth

2 tablespoons honey

¾ cup water

1 teaspoon cider vinegar

2 tablespoons raisins

1 teaspoon unsalted butter or
margarine

This handy kitchen tool simultaneously cores the apple and cuts it into wedges.

Welcome autumn—the glorious season of apples—with this tangy turkey sauté. You cook the apples with the skins on, so for extra color, use a selection of apples ranging from red to green to yellow. Try Empires, Granny Smiths and Golden Delicious, or Cortlands, Newtown Pippins and Gravensteins.

1 In a shallow bowl or pie plate, mix the flour, cumin, pepper, salt and cinnamon. Dredge the turkey in the flour mixture, patting it into the surface; reserve the excess flour mixture.

2 In a large, heavy no-stick skillet, warm the oil over medium-high heat. Add the turkey and sauté for 2 to 3 minutes per side, or until golden brown and cooked through. Transfer the turkey to a platter and cover loosely with foil to keep warm.

3 Add the apples, ½ cup of the broth and 1 tablespoon of the honey to the skillet. Cook over medium heat for 8 to 10 minutes, or until the apples are tender and nicely glazed, but not mushy; turn the apples frequently and scrape any brown bits from the bottom of the skillet. Remove the skillet from the heat. Spoon the apples over the turkey.

4 In a medium bowl, combine the reserved seasoned flour, remaining ¼ cup broth, remaining 1 tablespoon honey, the water and vinegar, and whisk until smooth. Pour this mixture into the skillet and bring to a boil over medium-heat, stirring constantly. Stir in the raisins. Simmer, stirring frequently, for 2 minutes, or until the sauce is thickened.

5 Stir in the butter or margarine, then remove the skillet from the heat. Pour the sauce over the turkey and apples.

Preparation time 15 minutes • **Total time** 40 minutes • **Per serving** 301 calories, 5.6 g. fat (18% of calories), 1.3 g. saturated fat, 73 mg. cholesterol, 378 mg. sodium, 2.7 g. dietary fiber, 32 mg. calcium, 2 mg. iron, 6 mg. vitamin C, 0 mg. beta-carotene
Serves 4

ON THE MENU
Serve the turkey and apples with broad noodles and broccoli.

KITCHEN TIPS
If honey becomes crystallized, set the jar in hot water for 10 to 15 minutes.

HOT-AND-SOUR TURKEY STIR-FRY

1 cup uncooked converted white rice

2½ cups water

8 ounces turkey breast cutlets, cut into thin strips

2 tablespoons grated fresh ginger

2 tablespoons dry sherry or defatted chicken broth

1 tablespoon plus 1 teaspoon reduced-sodium soy sauce

2 garlic cloves, crushed through a press

2 teaspoons granulated sugar

½ teaspoon ground white pepper

¼ teaspoon crushed red pepper flakes

⅛ teaspoon salt

1 tablespoon plus 1 teaspoon olive oil

4 cups broccoli florets

1 large red bell pepper, cut into thin strips

8 ounces shiitake or white button mushrooms, cut into thick slices (if using shiitakes, stem them)

½ cup defatted chicken broth

1 tablespoon cornstarch dissolved in 2 tablespoons rice vinegar

Sticklers for tradition will want to use a wok for this stir-fry, but a heavy skillet works perfectly well. The centuries-old design of the wok is perfect for stir-frying: Its sloping sides allow the food to be easily tossed and mixed, particularly if you use the traditional long-handled utensil that is a cross between a spoon and a spatula.

1 Combine the rice and 2 cups of the water in a heavy medium saucepan, and bring to a boil over high heat. Reduce the heat to low, cover and cook for 20 minutes, or until the rice is tender and the liquid is absorbed. Remove from the heat and set aside, covered.

2 While the rice is cooking, place the turkey strips in a shallow bowl. In a cup, combine the ginger, sherry or broth, soy sauce, garlic, sugar, white pepper, red pepper flakes and salt. Toss the turkey with 2 tablespoons of the ginger mixture.

3 In a large, deep no-stick skillet, warm 1½ teaspoons of the oil over high heat. Spread the turkey strips in the skillet and stir-fry for 2 to 3 minutes, or until the turkey is lightly browned and cooked through. Transfer the turkey to a plate.

4 Heat the remaining 2½ teaspoons oil in the skillet. Add the broccoli, bell peppers, mushrooms and the remaining ginger mixture, and stir-fry for 2 to 3 minutes, or until the peppers are crisp-tender and the broccoli is bright green.

5 Add the broth and the remaining ½ cup water to the skillet, and bring to a boil. Reduce the heat to medium-low, cover and simmer for 3 to 4 minutes, or until the broccoli is crisp-tender.

6 Increase the heat to high and stir in the turkey and any juices that have collected on the plate. Stir in the cornstarch mixture and bring to a boil, stirring constantly until the sauce is thickened. Serve the stir-fry over the rice.

Preparation time 20 minutes • **Total time** 40 minutes • **Per serving** 375 calories, 5.9 g. fat (14% of calories), 0.8 g. saturated fat, 35 mg. cholesterol, 459 mg. sodium, 6.5 g. dietary fiber, 102 mg. calcium, 4 mg. iron, 144 mg. vitamin C, 2 mg. beta-carotene • **Serves 4**

❧ ❧ ❧

Chicken with Ginger-Mustard Sauce

1 **pound thin-sliced chicken breast cutlets**

½ **teaspoon freshly ground black pepper**

¼ **teaspoon ground ginger**

⅛ **teaspoon salt**

2½ **teaspoons extra-virgin olive oil**

½ **cup defatted chicken broth**

1½ **teaspoons cornstarch, dissolved in ¼ cup cold water**

2 **teaspoons grated fresh ginger**

2 **teaspoons coarse Dijon mustard**

¼ **teaspoon dry mustard**

3 **tablespoons light sour cream**

As you whisk the cornstarch mixture into the skillet, the sauce will thicken and become glossy.

There's more than one way to make a cream sauce, as every health- and flavor-conscious cook should know. One French recipe for mustard sauce calls for 1½ cups of heavy cream and a few tablespoons of butter, plus the pan juices from roasted pork that has been basted with butter and lard. In a simple but significant transformation, this ginger-mustard sauce is made in the skillet after you sauté skinless chicken in just 2½ teaspoons of oil; the cornstarch and the prepared and dry mustards thicken the sauce, with light sour cream as a last-minute enrichment.

1 Season the chicken on both sides with the pepper, ground ginger and salt.

2 In a large, heavy no-stick skillet, warm the oil over medium-high heat. Add the chicken and sauté for 2 to 3 minutes per side, or just until browned and cooked through. Transfer the chicken to a platter and cover loosely with foil to keep warm.

3 Whisk the broth, cornstarch mixture, fresh ginger, Dijon mustard and dry mustard into the skillet. Place over medium-high heat and bring to a boil, whisking constantly until the sauce thickens. Remove the skillet from the heat.

4 Pour any chicken juices that have collected on the platter into the sauce and whisk in the sour cream. Spoon the sauce over the chicken.

Preparation time 10 minutes • **Total time** 25 minutes • **Per serving** 181 calories, 6.2 g. fat (31% of calories), 1.5 g. saturated fat, 70 mg. cholesterol, 342 mg. sodium, 0 g. dietary fiber, 16 mg. calcium, 1 mg. iron, 1 mg. vitamin C, 0 mg. beta-carotene
Serves 4

❧   ❧   ❧

KITCHEN TIPS

Cornstarch, a superfine flour made from the endosperm of the corn kernel, can thicken sauces without adding fat. Here are a few points to remember when cooking with cornstarch. If you stir the starch directly into hot liquid, it will almost certainly form lumps. To prevent this, combine the cornstarch with cold liquid (such as the water used here) and then add the mixture to the hot (not boiling) liquid. Whisk or stir constantly but gently as the cornstarch mixture is added and afterward: Too-vigorous beating—or too-high heat—will defeat the thickening power of the cornstarch.

CHICKEN CACCIATORE WITH RICE

¾ cup uncooked converted white rice

1½ cups water

1 tablespoon olive oil

1 medium onion, diced

2 garlic cloves, minced

8 ounces small fresh mushrooms, quartered

1 medium red bell pepper, cut into large dice

¾ teaspoon freshly ground black pepper

½ teaspoon dried oregano, crumbled

½ teaspoon dried tarragon, crumbled

⅛ teaspoon salt

¼ cup dry white wine or defatted chicken broth

1 can (28 ounces) tomatoes in purée, drained, ½ cup of purée reserved

2 tablespoons no-salt-added tomato paste

12 ounces skinless, boneless chicken thighs, cut into ½-inch pieces

Eating poultry without the skin eliminates much of its fat content; when you roast, broil or bake chicken, you can leave the skin on during cooking and remove it before you eat. However, when you stew or braise, the fat will end up in the sauce unless you remove the skin before cooking. Making chicken cacciatore with skinless thighs saves more than four grams of fat per serving.

1 Combine the rice and water in a heavy medium saucepan and bring to a boil over high heat. Reduce the heat to low, cover and simmer for 20 minutes, or until the rice is tender and the liquid is absorbed. Remove from the heat and set aside, covered (the rice will stay warm for a long time.)

2 Meanwhile, in a large, heavy no-stick skillet, warm the oil over medium-high heat. Add the onions and garlic, and stir to coat well with the oil. Stir in the mushrooms, bell peppers, black pepper, oregano, tarragon and salt; sauté, tossing the vegetables, for 3 minutes, or until they start to soften. Stir in the wine or broth and bring to a simmer. Reduce the heat to medium-low, cover and cook, stirring occasionally, for 4 to 5 minutes longer, or until the vegetables are tender.

3 Meanwhile, coarsely chop the tomatoes.

4 Add the chopped tomatoes with their reserved purée and the tomato paste to the skillet. Increase the heat to high and bring to a boil, stirring frequently. Reduce the heat to medium-low, cover and simmer, stirring occasionally, for 5 minutes. Uncover the pot and simmer for 5 minutes longer, or until the flavors are blended.

5 Stir in the chicken and simmer, uncovered, stirring occasionally, for 6 to 8 minutes longer, or until the chicken is cooked through. Serve the chicken cacciatore over the rice.

Preparation time 15 minutes • **Total time** 50 minutes • **Per serving** 368 calories, 7.3 g. fat (18% of calories), 1.4 g. saturated fat, 71 mg. cholesterol, 470 mg. sodium, 2.8 g. dietary fiber, 127 mg. calcium, 4 mg. iron, 78 mg. vitamin C, 2 mg. beta-carotene • **Serves 4**

SAUTÉED CHICKEN WITH PLUMS

1 teaspoon grated lemon zest

½ teaspoon dried thyme, crumbled

¼ teaspoon salt

¼ teaspoon freshly ground
black pepper

⅛ teaspoon ground nutmeg

1 pound skinless, boneless
chicken breast halves (4)

1 tablespoon olive oil

12 ounces ripe plums, cut into
½-inch wedges

⅓ cup apple juice

⅓ cup defatted chicken broth

3 tablespoons plum jam

1 teaspoon fresh lemon juice

2 teaspoons cornstarch, dissolved
in 1 tablespoon cold water

Fresh thyme sprigs for garnish
(optional)

To serve the chicken as it is shown on the cover of this book, cut each chicken breast crosswise into six or seven slices. Fan the slices over a pool of sauce on the plate, then top with some of the plums.

Different varieties of plums will subtly alter the taste of this sauté: Santa Rosas and Casselmans are on the tart side, while Tragedy and Queen Ann plums are sweeter. Be careful not to overcook the plums; the time required will depend on their type and ripeness. If you'd like to present this dish as it is shown on the cover, follow the directions at left for slicing and saucing the chicken breasts.

1 In a cup, mix the lemon zest, thyme, salt, pepper and nutmeg. Sprinkle the mixture over both sides of the chicken.

2 In a large, heavy no-stick skillet, warm the oil over medium-high heat. Add the chicken, skinned side down, and reduce the heat to medium. Sauté for 4 to 6 minutes per side, or until cooked through. Transfer the chicken to a clean plate and cover loosely with foil to keep warm.

3 Add the plums to the skillet and sauté for 1 minute, or until they start to soften. Add the apple juice, broth, jam and lemon juice, and bring to a boil. Reduce the heat to medium-low, cover the skillet and simmer, stirring occasionally, for 2 to 3 minutes, or until the plums have softened; be careful not to let them turn mushy.

4 Pour any chicken juices that have collected on the plate into the skillet and then stir in the cornstarch mixture. Increase the heat to medium and cook, stirring constantly but gently to keep the plums intact, until the mixture comes to a boil and thickens. Remove the skillet from the heat.

5 Place the chicken breasts on dinner plates. Spoon the plums and sauce over the chicken and garnish with thyme sprigs, if desired.

Preparation time 12 minutes • **Total time** 30 minutes • **Per serving** 254 calories, 5.5 g. fat (19% of calories), 0.9 g. saturated fat, 66 mg. cholesterol, 297 mg. sodium, 1.9 g. dietary fiber, 27 mg. calcium, 1.3 mg. iron, 20 mg. vitamin C, 0.2 mg. beta-carotene • **Serves 4**

❧ ❧ ❧

ON THE MENU
Serve the chicken with couscous or rice, topped with a little of the plum sauce.

Carrot sticks or sliced yellow summer squash or zucchini, simply steamed, make a colorful complement to the chicken.

Pepper Chicken with Penne

3 garlic cloves, crushed through a press

¾ teaspoon coarsely ground black pepper

¼ teaspoon crushed red pepper flakes

¼ teaspoon salt

12 ounces skinless, boneless chicken breast halves, cut crosswise into thin slices

1 tablespoon olive oil, preferably extra-virgin

8 ounces penne pasta

1 medium red bell pepper, cut into thin strips

1 medium green bell pepper, cut into thin strips

1 medium yellow bell pepper, cut into thin strips

1 can (16 ounces) tomatoes in juice, drained and coarsely chopped

½ cup defatted chicken broth

There are no less than five peppers in this recipe—black pepper, red pepper flakes and red, green and yellow bell peppers. Of course, the bell peppers are all the same vegetable, but they differ slightly in flavor; the yellow and red peppers are sweeter than the green. If all three colors are not available, feel free to prepare the recipe using whatever bell peppers are in your market.

1 Bring a large covered pot of water to a boil over high heat.

2 Meanwhile, on a plate, mix the garlic, black pepper, red pepper flakes and salt; add the chicken and toss until well coated.

3 In a large no-stick skillet, warm 1½ teaspoons of the oil over high heat. Add the chicken and stir-fry for 2 to 3 minutes, or until lightly browned and cooked through. Transfer the chicken to a clean plate.

4 Add the pasta to the boiling water and return to a boil. Cook for 10 to 12 minutes, or according to package directions until al dente. Drain the pasta in a colander and transfer to a warmed serving bowl.

5 Add the remaining 1½ teaspoons oil to the skillet and warm over medium-high heat. Add all the bell peppers to the skillet and stir-fry for 3 to 4 minutes, or until the peppers start to soften and brown. Add the tomatoes and broth, and bring to a boil. Reduce the heat to low, cover and simmer, stirring occasionally, for 3 to 4 minutes, or until the peppers are very tender.

6 Return the chicken to the skillet, adding any juices that have collected on the plate. Cover the skillet and simmer for 3 minutes, or until the chicken is heated through and the flavors are blended. Pour the chicken mixture over the pasta and toss to mix.

Preparation time 20 minutes • **Total time** 40 minutes • **Per serving** 380 calories, 6 g. fat (14% of calories), 1 g. saturated fat, 49 mg. cholesterol, 504 mg. sodium, 3.2 g. dietary fiber, 62 mg. calcium, 4 mg. iron, 87 mg. vitamin C, 1 mg. beta-carotene • **Serves 4**

SOUTHWESTERN CHICKEN SAUTÉ

1 tablespoon chili powder

1¼ teaspoons ground cumin

¼ teaspoon salt

⅛ teaspoon ground red pepper

1 pound skinless, boneless
chicken breast halves (4)

2 teaspoons olive oil

½ cup defatted chicken broth

1 tablespoon cider vinegar

8 ounces ripe plum tomatoes,
diced

1 cup frozen corn kernels

1 can (4 ounces) mild green
chilies, rinsed and drained

¼ cup chopped fresh cilantro

1 lime, cut into wedges

Cilantro, or Chinese parsley, looks something like flat-leaf parsley. If you're not sure which is which, crush a leaf between your fingers—the aroma of cilantro is unmistakable.

The chicken is topped with a super-chunky warm "salsa" made with tomatoes, corn and chilies. A quick chili rub gets the chicken off to a flavorful start, and more of the chili mixture goes into the sauce. Chili powder is a spice blend, but ground red pepper is unadulterated "heat": Leave it out if you want a milder dish.

1 In a cup, mix the chili powder, cumin, salt and pepper. Rub both sides of the chicken breasts with 1 tablespoon of the spice mixture.

2 In a large, heavy no-stick skillet, warm the oil over medium-high heat. Add the chicken and sauté for 2 to 3 minutes per side, or until the spice coating is browned and the surface of the chicken is opaque. (The chicken will finish cooking later.) Transfer the chicken to a clean plate.

3 Add the broth, vinegar and the remaining spice mixture to the skillet; increase the heat to high and bring to a boil, stirring to get up the browned bits from the bottom of the skillet. Boil for 1 to 2 minutes, or until the liquid is slightly reduced.

4 Return the chicken to the skillet, adding any juices that have collected on the plate. Add the tomatoes, corn and chilies, and bring to a simmer. Spoon the corn and tomato mixture over the chicken; reduce the heat to medium, cover and simmer, stirring once or twice, for 5 minutes, or until the chicken is cooked through and the flavors are blended. Transfer the chicken and vegetables to a serving dish and sprinkle with the cilantro.

5 Serve the chicken and vegetables with the lime wedges.

Preparation time 10 minutes • **Total time** 30 minutes • **Per serving** 214 calories, 4.9 g. fat (20% of calories), 0.7 g. saturated fat, 66 mg. cholesterol, 410 mg. sodium, 2.6 g. dietary fiber, 37 mg. calcium, 2 mg. iron, 21 mg. vitamin C, 0.7 mg. beta-carotene • **Serves 4**

ৡ৳   ৡ৳   ৡ৳

ON THE MENU
The perfect partner for the chicken and vegetables is a corn or flour tortilla or a slice of cornbread. And serve a salad of chilled blanched green beans and ripe tomato wedges with a vinaigrette dressing.

In the Oven

❧ ❧ ❧

BAKED AND BROILED
POULTRY DISHES WITH THE
FASCINATING FLAVORS
OF ITALY, INDIA, JAPAN AND
THE CARIBBEAN

Turkey Tonkatsu with Vegetables

1 teaspoon vegetable oil

1 large egg white

3 tablespoons water

½ cup unseasoned dry bread crumbs

1 tablespoon plus ½ teaspoon grated fresh ginger

1 tablespoon reduced-sodium soy sauce

1 pound thin-sliced turkey breast cutlets (4)

3 cups cauliflower florets

2 cups thinly sliced carrots

3 tablespoons rice vinegar

1 tablespoon honey

¼ teaspoon salt

¼ teaspoon crushed red pepper flakes

¼ teaspoon freshly ground black pepper

2 scallions, thinly sliced on the diagonal

2 teaspoons dark sesame oil

Tonkatsu means "pork cutlet," but this turkey variation is lighter than the original. The crumbed cutlets are usually fried in oil; baking them in the oven cuts lots of fat from the dish. The pickled vegetables are *sunomono*—Japanese for "vinegared things."

1 Brush a jelly-roll pan with the vegetable oil.

2 In a shallow bowl, using a fork, beat the egg white and 1 tablespoon of the water until frothy. Place the bread crumbs on a plate.

3 On another plate, mix 1½ teaspoons of the ginger with the soy sauce. Dip both sides of each turkey cutlet into the soy-sauce mixture. Dip the cutlets into the egg white, let the excess drip off, then dredge in the bread crumbs, pressing the crumbs into the surface. Arrange the turkey in a single layer in the prepared pan. Cover with a sheet of wax paper and set aside.

4 Preheat the oven to 425°.

5 In a medium saucepan, bring 1 inch of water to a boil over high heat. Add the cauliflower and carrots, and return to a boil. Cook for 4 to 6 minutes, or until the vegetables are crisp-tender. Drain in a colander and transfer to a serving bowl.

6 In the same saucepan, combine the remaining 2 teaspoons ginger, the vinegar, honey, salt, red pepper flakes, black pepper and remaining 2 tablespoons water, and bring to a boil over high heat, stirring.

7 Add half the scallions to the bowl of vegetables, then pour on the hot dressing and toss to mix; place the bowl in the freezer to chill.

8 Drizzle the sesame oil over the turkey and bake for 5 minutes. Turn and bake for 5 minutes longer, or until browned, crisp and cooked through. Cut the turkey diagonally into strips. Garnish the pickled vegetables with the remaining scallions and serve with the turkey.

Preparation time 15 minutes • **Total time** 30 minutes • **Per serving** 280 calories, 5.1 g. fat (16% of calories), 0.9 g. saturated fat, 70 mg. cholesterol, 505 mg. sodium, 4.3 g. dietary fiber, 88 mg. calcium, 3 mg. iron, 60 mg. vitamin C, 0.9 mg. beta-carotene • **Serves 4**

CRISPY CHICKEN WITH NECTARINE SALSA

- 1 large egg white
- 2 tablespoons plus 1 teaspoon fresh lime juice
- ½ cup unseasoned dry bread crumbs
- 1½ teaspoons chili powder
- 1¼ teaspoons ground cumin
- ¼ teaspoon salt
- 1 pound skinless, boneless chicken breast halves (4)
- 12 ounces ripe nectarines, diced
- ½ cup finely diced red bell peppers
- 2 tablespoons chopped fresh cilantro
- 1 tablespoon minced red onion
- 1 tablespoon honey
- ½ teaspoon minced, seeded pickled jalapeño pepper
- ⅛ teaspoon freshly ground black pepper
- 2 teaspoons olive oil

Peruse the menus of the country's trendiest restaurants and you'll find salsas made with pineapples, mangoes, cranberries, bananas, and just about any other fruit you can think of. This sweet-hot nectarine-and-jalapeño salsa is the ideal companion for crisp-crusted chicken breasts.

1 Spray a jelly-roll pan with no-stick spray.

2 In a shallow bowl or pie plate, using a fork, lightly beat the egg white with 1 tablespoon of the lime juice until frothy. In another shallow bowl, mix the bread crumbs, chili powder, 1 teaspoon of the cumin and the salt. One at a time, dip the chicken breasts into the egg white, letting the excess drip off, then roll the chicken in the crumbs, pressing them into the surface. Place the chicken breasts, skinned-side up, on the prepared pan. Set the chicken aside, uncovered.

3 Preheat the oven to 450°.

4 In a medium bowl, combine the nectarines, bell peppers, cilantro, onions, honey, jalapeño, black pepper, the remaining 1 tablespoon plus 1 teaspoon lime juice and remaining ¼ teaspoon cumin. Cover and set aside.

5 Drizzle the chicken evenly with the oil and bake for 10 minutes. Turn the chicken and bake for 5 minutes longer, or until crisp, lightly browned, and cooked through.

6 Serve the chicken with the nectarine salsa.

Preparation time 20 minutes • **Total time** 35 minutes • **Per serving** 257 calories, 5.1 g. fat (18% of calories), 0.8 g. saturated fat, 66 mg. cholesterol, 283 mg. sodium, 2.3 g. dietary fiber, 51 mg. calcium, 2 mg. iron, 32 mg. vitamin C, 1 mg. beta-carotene
Serves 4

SUBSTITUTION
Use peaches if nectarines are not available. Or substitute unsweetened frozen peach slices when the fresh fruits are out of season.

FOOD FACT
Nectarines and peaches are closely related, and the two fruits have been cross-bred to produce sweetier, tastier peaches and bigger nectarines.

CHICKEN-VEGETABLE PACKETS

1 can (8 ounces) no-salt-added tomato sauce

2 tablespoons grated Parmesan cheese

1 tablespoon balsamic vinegar

½ teaspoon freshly ground black pepper

½ teaspoon dried basil

⅛ teaspoon salt

8 slices (¼ inch thick) Spanish onion

8 rings (¼ inch thick) green bell pepper

12 ounces thin-sliced chicken breast cutlets, divided into 4 equal portions

8 slices (¼ inch thick) peeled eggplant

8 slices (¼ inch thick) ripe tomato

8 diagonal slices (½ ounce each) crusty French or Italian bread

1½ teaspoons extra-virgin olive oil

1 garlic clove, peeled and halved

3 ounces shredded part-skim mozzarella cheese

It is usually rather delicate foods—herbed fish fillets for instance—that are cooked in packets because this method treats food gently, steaming it with no basting or turning required. Here, more robust ingredients go in the foil packets, where the flavors blend to perfection. Garlic toasts are served on the side.

1 Preheat the oven to 450°. Tear off four 12-inch pieces of heavy-duty aluminum foil.

2 In a medium bowl, mix the tomato sauce, Parmesan, vinegar, black pepper, basil and salt.

3 Dividing the ingredients evenly, in the center of each piece of foil make a bed of onions and bell peppers. Place a portion of chicken on the vegetables, then top with a heaping tablespoon of the tomato sauce, some eggplant and tomatoes. Spoon the remaining sauce on top. Fold the foil up and over the chicken and vegetables, and seal it well.

4 Place the packets in a jelly-roll pan and bake for 30 to 35 minutes, or until the vegetables are tender and the chicken is cooked through (check by opening one of the packets).

5 After the packets have baked for 20 minutes, place the bread on a baking sheet and bake for about 5 minutes, or until toasted. Remove the baking sheet from the oven, drizzle each piece of toast with some of the oil and rub with the cut sides of the garlic clove.

6 Place each packet on a plate, open it up and sprinkle with some of the mozzarella. Loosely reclose the foil and let stand for 1 to 2 minutes to melt the cheese.

7 Open up the packets; transfer the vegetables and chicken to plates. Pour the juices around the vegetables and chicken, and place two garlic toasts on each plate.

Preparation time 15 minutes • **Total time** 50 minutes • **Per serving** 302 calories, 8.2 g. fat (24% of calories), 3.3 g. saturated fat, 64 mg. cholesterol, 462 mg. sodium, 3 g. dietary fiber, 230 mg. calcium, 2 mg. iron, 28 mg. vitamin C, 0.6 mg. beta-carotene • **Serves 4**

LEMON-ROSEMARY CHICKEN BREASTS

2 large lemons

2 tablespoons packed light brown sugar

1½ teaspoons coarsely chopped fresh rosemary leaves or ½ teaspoon dried

¼ teaspoon salt

¼ teaspoon freshly ground black pepper

2 pounds skinless bone-in chicken breast halves (4)

1 teaspoon cornstarch dissolved in 1 tablespoon cold water

Fresh rosemary sprigs for garnish (optional)

Here's a quick dinner that you can put together even when there's no time to shop. You can keep all the ingredients on hand, including the rosemary, which will last in the refrigerator for up to ten days. Of course, you can use dried rosemary instead of fresh. If you're substituting the dried herb, crumble it between your fingers to release its fragrance.

1 Preheat the oven to 400°. Spray a 9 x 13-inch baking pan with no-stick spray.

2 Grate 2 teaspoons of zest from one lemon, then halve the lemon and squeeze 3 tablespoons of juice from it into a shallow medium bowl. Cut the other lemon into thin slices, discarding the ends.

3 Add the lemon zest, sugar, rosemary, salt and pepper to the bowl of lemon juice and whisk to blend. One at time, dip the chicken breasts into the lemon mixture, turning to coat both sides.

4 Arrange the chicken breasts, skinned side up, in the prepared pan and place some of the lemon slices on top of each. (If any of the lemon mixture remains in the bowl, spoon it over the chicken.) Bake, basting twice with the pan juices, for 25 to 30 minutes, or until the chicken is cooked through.

5 Transfer the chicken to plates. Pour the pan juices into a small saucepan, stir in the cornstarch mixture and bring to a boil over medium heat, stirring constantly until thickened. Spoon the pan juices over the chicken. Garnish with rosemary sprigs, if desired.

Preparation time 5 minutes • **Total time** 35 minutes • **Per serving** 232 calories, 2.5 g. fat (10% of calories), 1 g. saturated fat, 101 mg. cholesterol, 253 mg. sodium, 0 g. dietary fiber, 47 mg. calcium, 2 mg. iron, 30 mg. vitamin C, 0 mg. beta-carotene
Serves 4

❧ ❧ ❧

KITCHEN TIPS
Wrap fresh rosemary in a small plastic bag and store it in the crisper drawer of the refrigerator.

ON THE MENU
Steamed green beans or yellow wax beans (or a mix of the two) and crisp rolls make this meal complete.

BAKED CHICKEN BARBECUE

1 medium red bell pepper, cut into thin strips

1 medium green bell pepper, cut into thin strips

1 small onion, halved and sliced

2 garlic cloves, crushed through a press

2 tablespoons defatted chicken broth

2 tablespoons water

2 cans (8 ounces each) no-salt-added tomato sauce

¼ cup raisins

3 tablespoons molasses

1 tablespoon plus 1 teaspoon cider vinegar

½–1 teaspoon hot-pepper sauce

1 teaspoon dry mustard

½ teaspoon freshly ground black pepper

¼ teaspoon salt

1 pound 12 ounces skinned bone-in chicken legs, thighs and drumsticks separated (4 whole legs)

Oven-baked barbecue is a Southern specialty quite distinct from either suburban backyard grilling or large-scale open-pit smoking. In this adaptation of the recipe, chicken legs take the place of the more usual short ribs; the chicken is baked in a tangy tomato sauce made with raisins, molasses and vinegar. Don't worry too much about overcooking the chicken: Most people prefer oven-barbecued meats "falling off the bone" tender.

1 Preheat the oven to 425°. Spray a roasting pan with no-stick spray.

2 In a heavy medium saucepan, combine the bell peppers, onions, garlic, broth and water; bring to a boil over high heat. Reduce the heat to medium; cover and simmer, stirring several times, for 5 minutes, or until the vegetables are crisp-tender.

3 Stir in the tomato sauce, raisins, molasses, vinegar, hot-pepper sauce, mustard, black pepper and salt; increase the heat to medium-high and bring to a boil.

4 Place the chicken pieces in the prepared pan. Spoon the sauce over the chicken and toss to coat the chicken.

5 Bake the chicken, turning the pieces and basting occasionally with the sauce, for 25 to 35 minutes, or until the chicken is cooked through and very tender.

Preparation time 10 minutes • **Total time** 45 minutes • **Per serving** 299 calories, 6.2 g. fat (19% of calories), 1.3 g. saturated fat, 108 mg. cholesterol, 340 mg. sodium, 3.3 g. dietary fiber, 66 mg. calcium, 4 mg. iron, 77 mg. vitamin C, 2 mg. beta-carotene
Serves 4

ON THE MENU
Cornbread and coleslaw are the classic accompaniments for barbecue. You could lighten up the coleslaw with a yogurt dressing, though, and add some shredded broccoli and red bell pepper to the standard cabbage and carrots. Iced tea and lemonade are the perfect drinks.

MAKE AHEAD
Cook the chicken a day ahead, cover with foil and refrigerate. Reheat covered, adding a little water if necessary.

FOR A CHANGE
Use quartered bone-in chicken breasts instead of the thighs.

JERK CHICKEN WITH MANGO

2 fresh jalapeño peppers, halved and partially seeded

½ small onion, halved

2 garlic cloves, peeled

1 slice (¼ inch thick) peeled fresh ginger

1 tablespoon paprika

1 tablespoon defatted chicken broth

2 teaspoons olive oil

2 teaspoons distilled white vinegar

1½ teaspoons dried thyme

1 teaspoon ground allspice

½ teaspoon freshly ground black pepper

¼ teaspoon salt

4 skinless bone-in chicken breast halves (2 pounds)

1 ripe mango, peeled and diced

1 tablespoon chopped fresh mint

Scallions and mint sprigs for garnish (optional)

A South American Indian word for strips of cured meat—*charqui*—may have given rise to the word "jerk," which is used in the Caribbean to describe meat that is rubbed with spices and then grilled, baked or smoked. For a lavish presentation, buy an extra mango to garnish the platter: Halve the unpeeled fruit, score the flesh into cubes and turn each half "inside out."

1 Preheat the oven to 450°. Spray a 9 x 13-inch baking pan with no-stick spray.

2 In a food processor, combine the jalapeños, onions, garlic, ginger, paprika, broth, oil, vinegar, thyme, allspice, black pepper and salt, and process until very finely chopped, stopping the machine a few times to scrape down the sides of the container.

3 Using a rubber spatula, spread the jalapeño mixture on both sides of the chicken breasts. Place them, skinned side up, in the prepared pan.

4 Bake the chicken for 30 to 35 minutes, or until lightly browned and cooked through. Place the chicken on plates and scatter the diced mango on top. Sprinkle the mango with the mint. Garnish with scallions and mint sprigs, if desired.

Preparation time 10 minutes • **Total time** 45 minutes • **Per serving** 268 calories, 5.1 g. fat (17% of calories), 1 g. saturated fat, 101 mg. cholesterol, 268 mg. sodium, 1 g. dietary fiber, 51 mg. calcium, 3 mg. iron, 38 mg. vitamin C, 2 mg. beta-carotene
Serves 4

ॐ ॐ ॐ

To prepare the mango used in the topping, first pare it with a vegetable peeler.

Slice off most of the flesh in two halves, cutting on either side of the flat pit.

Cut off the flesh that remains around the pit, then dice the mango.

TURKEY YAKITORI WITH VEGETABLES

1 **pound thin-sliced turkey breast cutlets**

3 **tablespoons no-sugar-added apricot spread**

2 **tablespoons low-sodium ketchup**

1 **tablespoon plus 2 teaspoons reduced-sodium soy sauce**

1 **tablespoon grated fresh ginger**

1 **large garlic clove, crushed**

2 **teaspoons dark sesame oil**

½ **teaspoon cider vinegar**

¼ **teaspoon hot-pepper sauce**

2 **medium red bell peppers, cut into 1½-inch squares**

12 **scallions, root ends trimmed, green tops left on**

Thread the strips of turkey ribbonwise onto the wooden skewers.

Whole restaurants in Japan are devoted to *yakitori*—skewered meats cooked over a charcoal fire—which are eaten either as snacks or, served with rice, as a main dish. Here, whole scallions and generous pieces of red pepper are grilled alongside skewered strips of turkey. You'll need eight 12-inch bamboo skewers for this recipe: Soak them in cold water for at least half an hour to prevent them from charring under the broiler.

1 Preheat the broiler. Spray the broiler-pan rack with no-stick spray.

2 Cut the turkey into eight 1-inch-wide strips.

3 In a medium bowl, combine the apricot spread, ketchup, soy sauce, ginger, garlic, oil, vinegar and hot-pepper sauce; stir well. Add the turkey strips and turn them until well coated with the sauce. Thread each strip on a 12-inch bamboo skewer and set aside.

4 Add the bell pepper squares to the sauce and toss until well coated. Arrange the peppers in a single layer on one side of the broiler pan. Place the scallions in the sauce (thin it with 1 teaspoon of water if necessary) and turn them to coat. Place the scallions on the other side of the broiler pan and broil the vegetables 5 to 6 inches from the heat for 5 to 6 minutes, or until the scallions are tender and very lightly charred.

5 Transfer the scallions to a warm platter and cover loosely with a sheet of foil to keep warm. Turn the peppers, spread them out a bit on the pan and broil for 5 to 6 minutes longer, or until tender and somewhat charred. Transfer the pepper squares to the platter.

6 Place the skewers of turkey on the broiler pan. Cover the exposed ends of the skewers with a strip of foil so they do not burn. Broil the turkey without turning for 4 to 5 minutes, or until cooked through. Serve the turkey with the bell peppers and scallions.

Preparation time 15 minutes • **Total time** 45 minutes • **Per serving** 213 calories, 3.2 g. fat (13% of calories), 0.6 g. saturated fat, 70 mg. cholesterol, 377 mg. sodium, 1.7 g. dietary fiber, 54 mg. calcium, 2 mg. iron, 79 mg. vitamin C, 1.4 mg. beta-carotene • **Serves 4**

❧ ❧ ❧

TANDOORI CHICKEN

1¼ cups nonfat yogurt

1 garlic clove, crushed through a press

1 teaspoon ground cumin

½ teaspoon ground coriander

¼ teaspoon freshly ground black pepper

¼ teaspoon salt

¼ teaspoon ground ginger

¼ teaspoon ground turmeric

Large pinch of ground red pepper

½ cup diced fresh tomatoes

½ cup diced peeled cucumbers

¼ cup minced fresh cilantro, plus cilantro sprigs for garnish (optional)

1 pound skinned boneless chicken thighs (8)

¾ cup uncooked converted white rice

¾ cup water

¾ cup defatted chicken broth

From the urn-shaped brick-and-clay oven known as a *tandoor* come some of India's best-loved foods. A fire is built in the tandoor, and when the coals are white-hot, skewered meats are lowered into the oven. The intense heat cooks kebabs or a halved chicken with remarkable speed. Some Indian breads, such as *naan* and *roti*, are made by slapping portions of dough against the searing-hot inner walls of the tandoor, where they cook in about one minute.

1 Preheat the oven to 425°. Spray a 7 x 11-inch baking pan with no-stick spray.

2 In a medium bowl, mix the yogurt with the garlic, cumin, coriander, black pepper, salt, ginger, turmeric and red pepper. Transfer ⅔ cup of the yogurt mixture to another medium bowl and stir in the tomatoes, cucumbers and minced cilantro; cover and refrigerate.

3 Add the chicken thighs to the remaining yogurt mixture and toss to coat well. Arrange the chicken in a single layer, skinned side up, in the prepared pan; spoon any remaining yogurt mixture over the chicken. Bake for 20 to 25 minutes, or until the chicken is cooked through.

4 Meanwhile, combine the rice, water and broth in a heavy medium saucepan; bring to a boil over high heat. Reduce the heat to low, cover and simmer for 20 minutes, or until the rice is tender and the liquid is absorbed.

5 Spread the rice on a platter and arrange the chicken thighs on top. Spoon the reserved yogurt-vegetable mixture over the chicken and rice; garnish with cilantro sprigs, if desired.

Preparation time 15 minutes • **Total time** 45 minutes • **Per serving** 322 calories, 5.4 g. fat (15% of calories), 1.3 g. saturated fat, 96 mg. cholesterol, 478 mg. sodium, 1 g. dietary fiber, 188 mg. calcium, 3 mg. iron, 11 mg. vitamin C, 0.1 mg. beta-carotene • **Serves 4**

FOODWAYS
In earlier times, chicken was rubbed with saffron and a natural coloring called cochineal to turn it a deep red in the tan-door. Today, artificial food coloring is sometimes added. In this version of tan-doori chicken, deep-yellow turmeric turns the chicken golden rather than red.

GRILLED GARLIC LIME GAME HENS

2 Cornish game hens (1½ pounds
   each), split

¼ cup plus 2 tablespoons fresh
   lime juice

1 tablespoon grated lime zest

3 garlic cloves, crushed
   through a press

1 teaspoon extra-virgin olive oil

¼ teaspoon salt

¼ teaspoon freshly ground black
   pepper

⅛ teaspoon crushed red pepper
   flakes

You'll discard the skin before eating these juicy game hens, but while the birds roast, the skin seals in the zesty marinade. Because the recipe is for the hens only, the ratio of calories from fat may seem high. You can restore the balance by serving the hens with a complex carbohydrate, such as rice, potatoes or couscous.

1 Place the hens in a shallow no-stick baking pan (or foil-lined pan) large enough to hold them in a single layer. In a small bowl, mix the lime juice, lime zest, garlic, oil, salt, black pepper and red pepper flakes.

2 Pour the mixture over the hens, rubbing it over both sides and especially under the skin. Cover and let stand for 10 minutes.

3 Meanwhile, preheat the broiler.

4 Broil the hens 5 to 6 inches from the heat for about 10 minutes per side, or until the hens are browned and the juices run clear, not pink, when the hens are pierced at the thigh with a sharp knife. Baste the hens with the pan juices while they are roasting.

5 Remove the skin from the hens before eating.

Preparation time 10 minutes • **Total time** 40 minutes • **Per serving** 253 calories, 10.2 g. fat (36% of calories), 2.6 g. saturated fat, 108 mg. cholesterol, 241 mg. sodium, 0 g. dietary fiber, 34 mg. calcium, 2 mg. iron, 9 mg. vitamin C, 0 mg. beta-carotene • **Serves 4**

❧ ❧ ❧

Use kitchen shears to split the Cornish hens down the backbone.

Then turn the birds over and split them along the breastbone.

In the Pot

❧ ❧ ❧

SIMMER UP A SOOTHING SOUP,

STEW, GUMBO OR CHOWDER,

OR A HEARTY ONE-DISH

MEAL WITH VEGETABLES, RICE

OR NOODLES

CHICKEN PAPRIKASH

2 tablespoons all-purpose flour

1 tablespoon sweet paprika

½ teaspoon freshly ground black pepper

¼ teaspoon dried basil, crumbled

⅛ teaspoon ground red pepper

⅛ teaspoon salt

1½ pounds skinless bone-in chicken breast halves (4)

2 teaspoons olive oil

2 large onions, thinly sliced

½ cup defatted chicken broth

½ cup sliced roasted red peppers (from a jar), rinsed and drained

1 cup crushed canned tomatoes

½ cup water

1 tablespoon no-salt-added tomato paste

6 ounces egg noodles

¼ cup nonfat sour cream

2 tablespoons snipped fresh chives or slivered scallions

Rosy red paprika is one of the defining ingredients of Hungarian cooking. Made by grinding dried red peppers to a fine powder, paprika ranges from mild (sweet) to hot. Imported Hungarian paprika, in red-green-and-white tins, is sold in many supermarkets.

1 In a shallow bowl or pie plate, mix the flour, paprika, black pepper, basil, red pepper and salt. Dredge the chicken breasts in the flour mixture. Set aside the excess dredging mixture.

2 In a Dutch oven or a large, heavy saucepan, warm the oil over medium-high heat. Add the chicken and cook for 2 minutes per side, or until lightly browned. Using tongs, transfer the chicken to a plate.

3 Add the onions to the pan; drizzle in 1 tablespoon of broth. Reduce the heat to medium and sauté for 10 to 12 minutes, or until the onions are tender and golden, gradually adding 3 tablespoons more broth.

4 Meanwhile, bring a covered pot of water to a boil over high heat.

5 Stir the roasted peppers and the reserved dredging mixture into the onions; sauté, stirring constantly, for 1 minute. Stir in the remaining ¼ cup broth, the tomatoes, water and tomato paste, and bring to a boil over high heat. Add the chicken and any juices that have collected on the plate; reduce the heat to medium-low, cover and simmer, stirring occasionally, for 20 minutes, or until the chicken is cooked through.

6 Meanwhile, add the noodles to the boiling water and return to a boil. Cook for 9 to 11 minutes, or according to package directions until al dente. Drain the noodles in a colander.

7 Remove the chicken from the pan. Add the noodles to the pan and toss quickly; spread the sauced noodles on a platter. Arrange the chicken breasts on the noodles, top with dollops of sour cream and sprinkle with the chives or scallions.

Preparation time 10 minutes • **Total time** 50 minutes • **Per serving** 467 calories, 7 g. fat (14% of calories), 1.3 g. saturated fat, 139 mg. cholesterol, 430 mg. sodium, 3.8 g. dietary fiber, 102 mg. calcium, 5 mg. iron, 43 mg. vitamin C, 1.4 mg. beta-carotene • **Serves 4**

❧ ❧ ❧

Spicy Red Bean and Chicken Soup

8 ounces skinless, boneless chicken breast halves, cut crosswise into ¼-inch-thick strips

1 medium green bell pepper, cut into thin strips

1 medium red onion, halved and thinly sliced

1 tablespoon plus 2 teaspoons chili powder

2 teaspoons olive oil

1 cup defatted chicken broth

1 can (19 ounces) red kidney beans, rinsed and drained

8 ounces small red or white potatoes, scrubbed and cut into ½-inch chunks

1¾ cups water

1 can (4 ounces) mild green chilies, rinsed and drained

1 medium ripe tomato (about 8 ounces), diced

3 tablespoons light sour cream

For a surprising contrast of tastes and textures, chili-rubbed chicken strips and vegetables are sautéed and placed atop the bowls of bean soup just before serving. If you think the amount of chili powder called for might be a bit too much for you, start with just a teaspoonful in the soup and add more as needed.

1 In a medium bowl, toss the chicken strips, bell peppers and onions with 2 teaspoons of the chili powder.

2 In a large, heavy saucepan, warm the oil over medium-high heat. Add the chicken, bell peppers and onions, and toss to coat well with the oil. Sauté, tossing, for 2 minutes, or until the chicken begins to turn white. Drizzle with 2 tablespoons of broth and sauté for 3 to 4 minutes longer, or until the chicken is cooked through and the vegetables tender. Transfer to a clean bowl and cover loosely with foil to keep the chicken moist.

3 In the same saucepan, combine the beans, potatoes, water, chilies, the remaining broth and remaining 1 tablespoon chili powder. Cover and bring to a boil over high heat. Reduce the heat to medium-low and simmer, stirring occasionally, for 12 to 15 minutes, or until the potatoes are tender.

4 Using a slotted spoon, transfer 1½ cups of the bean mixture to a bowl and mash it. Whisk this mixture back into the soup and return the saucepan to medium heat. Stir in the tomatoes and cook, stirring frequently, for 3 to 4 minutes, or just until the tomatoes are heated through.

5 Ladle the soup into large soup bowls and place some of the chicken and vegetables on top of each portion. Spoon a dollop of sour cream onto each serving of soup.

Preparation time 15 minutes • **Total time** 45 minutes • **Per serving** 297 calories, 6.5 g. fat (20% of calories), 1.3 g. saturated fat, 37 mg. cholesterol, 548 mg. sodium, 9.5 g. dietary fiber, 64 mg. calcium, 3 mg. iron, 45 mg. vitamin C, 0.9 mg. beta-carotene • **Serves 4**

TORTILLA SOUP WITH LIME

2 teaspoons olive oil

4 corn tortillas (6-inch), halved and cut into ¼-inch-wide strips

2¼ cups water

1¼ cups defatted chicken broth

12 ounces thin-sliced turkey breast cutlets, cut into ½-inch-thick strips

1 medium Spanish onion, halved and thinly sliced (about 2½ cups)

1 large red bell pepper, cut into thin strips

1 large fresh jalapeño pepper, minced

2¼ teaspoons ground cumin

¼ teaspoon dried oregano

½ cup frozen corn kernels

½ cup quartered cherry tomatoes

¼ cup chopped fresh cilantro

2 tablespoons fresh lime juice

½ ripe avocado, diced

Save the croutons or crackers for more pedestrian soups: This zesty bowl of turkey and vegetables is topped with crisped tortilla strips. Fresh jalapeño peppers give the soup a Tex-Mex kick (the method of preparing them is shown below). Remove all the seeds for a slightly milder flavor, or leave some in for serious heat. It's best to wear rubber gloves when handling the jalapeños or any other fresh chilies.

1 In a large, heavy saucepan, warm the oil over high heat. Add the tortillas and stir-fry them for 2 to 4 minutes, or until they are crisped and lightly browned on the edges. Transfer the tortillas to a plate.

2 In the saucepan, combine the water, broth, turkey strips, onions, bell peppers, jalapeños, cumin and oregano; cover and bring to a boil over high heat. Reduce the heat to medium-low and simmer for 10 minutes.

3 Stir in the corn and simmer for 5 minutes longer. Remove the pan from the heat and stir in the tomatoes, cilantro and lime juice.

4 Ladle the soup into bowls and top each portion with some of the avocado and the tortilla crisps.

Preparation time 15 minutes • **Total time** 40 minutes • **Per serving** 296 calories, 8.3 g. fat (25% of calories), 1.2 g. saturated fat, 53 mg. cholesterol, 408 mg. sodium, 4.4 g. dietary fiber, 105 mg. calcium, 3 mg. iron, 78 mg. vitamin C, 1.1 mg. beta-carotene • **Serves 4**

Trim the stem end from the jalapeño and halve the pepper lengthwise.

Scrape out some or all of the seeds and fibrous ribs—the source of the chili's heat.

CHICKEN, POTATO AND LEEK SOUP

2 large leeks

1¼ pounds all-purpose potatoes, scrubbed and cut into 1-inch chunks

2 cups water

1½ cups defatted chicken broth

2 medium cucumbers, peeled, halved, seeded and cut into ½-inch slices

1 medium onion, halved and sliced

2 garlic cloves, crushed through a press

¾ teaspoon freshly ground black pepper

½ teaspoon dried thyme

⅛ teaspoon salt

1 pound skinless, boneless chicken breast halves, cut into ½-inch dice

2 teaspoons unsalted butter or margarine

Dill sprigs for garnish (optional)

As delicious as this soup is hot, it's also good cold. Leave out the butter or margarine (which would congeal when the soup was chilled) and refrigerate the soup, covered, until thoroughly chilled. Stir in some buttermilk or plain yogurt just before serving and add some chopped fresh dill or other herbs, if you like.

1 Halve the leeks lengthwise and cut off the root ends and coarser part of the green tops. Hold the leeks under cold running water and wash thoroughly. Cut the leeks diagonally into 1-inch slices.

2 In a large, heavy saucepan, combine the leeks, potatoes, water, broth, cucumbers, onions, garlic, pepper, thyme and salt; cover and bring to a boil over high heat. Reduce the heat to medium-low and simmer, stirring once or twice, for 15 to 20 minutes, or until the potatoes are very tender.

3 Mash the vegetables slightly to thicken the soup, but leave it somewhat chunky.

4 Stir in the chicken and increase the heat to medium; cover and cook for 3 minutes longer, or until the chicken is cooked through.

5 Add the butter or margarine and stir just until melted. Ladle the soup into bowls and garnish with dill sprigs, if desired.

Preparation time 25 minutes • **Total time** 45 minutes • **Per serving** 334 calories, 4.3 g. fat (12% of calories), 1.6 g. saturated fat, 71 mg. cholesterol, 541 mg. sodium, 4.3 g. dietary fiber, 95 mg. calcium, 4 mg. iron, 51 mg. vitamin C, 0 mg. beta-carotene
Serves 4

FOR A CHANGE
Leave out the chicken and make a lighter vegetarian soup to serve as a first course.

SUBSTITUTION
If you can't get leeks, use a large bunch of scallions instead. You don't have to wash scallions as carefully as you do leeks: Just cut off the roots and trim the very tops of the leaves if they are dry or withered.

KITCHEN TIPS
To prepare the cucumbers, first peel them, then halve them lengthwise. Use a teaspoon to scoop out the seeds and then slice the cucumbers crosswise.

CHICKEN WITH SPRING VEGETABLES

1 cup defatted chicken broth

1 cup water

2 tablespoons dry white wine or additional chicken broth

2 garlic cloves, crushed through a press

1 bay leaf, preferably imported

½ teaspoon dried tarragon

¼ teaspoon freshly ground black pepper

⅛ teaspoon salt

1 pound skinless, boneless chicken breast halves (4)

2 large carrots, diagonally sliced

2 large celery stalks with leaves, sliced

12 ounces fresh asparagus spears, trimmed and diagonally sliced

½ cup frozen peas

½ cup diagonally sliced scallions

2 tablespoons cornstarch, dissolved in 2 tablespoons fresh lemon juice

Here's a version of chicken in the pot with a lighter touch: Instead of chicken thighs and hearty root vegetables, this dish combines chicken breasts with asparagus and peas. A little lemon juice accentuates the fresh, springlike flavors.

1 In a Dutch oven or large, heavy saucepan, combine the broth, water, wine or additional broth, garlic, bay leaf, tarragon, pepper and salt; cover and bring to a boil over high heat. Reduce the heat to medium-low and simmer for 5 minutes to blend the flavors.

2 Place the chicken breasts in the pan and scatter the carrots and celery over them. Increase the heat to medium-high and bring the liquid to a simmer. Reduce the heat to medium-low, cover and simmer slowly, turning the chicken once, for 10 to 12 minutes, or until the chicken is cooked through and the vegetables are tender.

3 With a slotted spoon, transfer the chicken and vegetables to 4 large heated soup plates. Remove and discard the bay leaf.

4 Increase the heat under the pan to high. Stir in the asparagus, peas and scallions, and bring to a boil. Simmer for 2 to 3 minutes, or until the asparagus is tender. Stir in the cornstarch mixture and return to a boil; cook, stirring constantly, until the broth is thickened. Remove the pan from the heat.

5 Ladle the thickened broth into the bowls of chicken and vegetables, and serve.

Preparation time 15 minutes • **Total time** 40 minutes • **Per serving** 211 calories, 2.0 g. fat (0.8% of calories), 0.4 g. saturated fat, 66 mg. cholesterol, 453 mg. sodium, 3.5 g. dietary fiber, 70 mg. calcium, 2 mg. iron, 32 mg. vitamin C, 8.9 mg. beta-carotene • **Serves 4**

FOR A CHANGE
Instead of frozen peas, use fresh or frozen snow peas, or small fresh sugar snap peas. The cooking time should be about the same.

KITCHEN TIPS
If you often use lemon juice, pick up a lemon "spigot." You twist the hollow tube into the lemon, squeeze as much juice as you need and then recap the spigot.

TEX-MEX TURKEY AND BLACK BEAN STEW

8 ounces skinless, boneless turkey breast, cut into chunks

1 tablespoon plus 1 teaspoon olive oil

1 medium green bell pepper, cut into ½-inch dice

1 medium red bell pepper, cut into ½-inch dice

1 large onion, coarsely diced

2 garlic cloves, minced

2 tablespoons chili powder

1 tablespoon ground cumin

¾ teaspoon freshly ground black pepper

½ teaspoon dried oregano, crumbled

2 cans (14½ ounces each) no-salt-added stewed tomatoes

1 can (16 ounces) black beans, rinsed and drained

¾ cup hot or medium prepared salsa

2 cups water

1 cup medium-coarse bulgur

¼ teaspoon hot pepper sauce

This family-pleasing turkey stew is a lot like chili, but it is served over bulgur—cracked, steamed kernels of wheat that make a satisfying alternative to rice. Using a food processor, you grind the skinless turkey breast yourself to be sure of the leanest, freshest meat. The job will go more smoothly if the turkey is well chilled.

1 Place the turkey in a food processor and pulse until coarsely chopped; set aside.

2 In a Dutch oven, warm 1 tablespoon of the oil over medium-high heat. Add the bell peppers, onions and garlic, and sauté for 5 minutes, or until the vegetables are crisp-tender.

3 Stir in the remaining 1 teaspoon oil, then stir in the ground turkey, chili powder, cumin, ground pepper and oregano (the mixture will be dry). Sauté, breaking up any clumps of meat with a spoon, for 1 to 2 minutes, or just until the ingredients are well mixed and the turkey starts to turn white.

4 Add the tomatoes, beans and salsa, and bring to a boil, breaking up the tomatoes with a spoon. Reduce the heat to medium-low, cover and simmer gently for 20 minutes.

5 Meanwhile, combine the water, bulgur and hot-pepper sauce in a heavy medium saucepan and bring to a boil over high heat. Reduce the heat to low, cover and simmer for 15 to 20 minutes, or until the bulgur is tender and the liquid has been absorbed.

6 Spoon the bulgur into bowls and ladle the stew over the bulgur.

Preparation time 15 minutes • **Total time** 45 minutes • **Per serving** 403 calories, 7.2 g. fat (16% of calories), 0.9 g. saturated fat, 35 mg. cholesterol, 574 mg. sodium, 17.1 g. dietary fiber, 154 mg. calcium, 6 mg. iron, 118 mg. vitamin C, 2 mg. beta-carotene • **Serves 4**

ON THE MENU
Serve the stew with warmed corn tortillas or oven-toast some tortilla triangles and use them as a garnish.

KITCHEN TIPS
To chill the turkey quickly for easier grinding, cut the meat into chunks and then place it in the freezer for a few minutes.

Chicken-Corn Chowder

1½ cups water

¾ cup defatted chicken broth

8 ounces skinless, boneless chicken breast halves, cut into ½-inch dice

8 ounces small red potatoes, cut into ½-inch dice

1 medium onion, diced

1 small green bell pepper, cut into ½-inch dice

1 small red bell pepper, cut into ½-inch dice

1 large celery stalk with leaves, diced

½ teaspoon dried thyme, crumbled

½ teaspoon freshly ground black pepper

¼ teaspoon salt

Kernels from 3 or 4 large ears fresh corn (about 1½ cups) or 1½ cups frozen corn kernels

3 tablespoons cornstarch

¾ cup 1% low-fat milk

¼ teaspoon hot-pepper sauce

3 tablespoons light sour cream

Fresh chives for garnish (optional)

A smooth, creamy broth is the foil for bright corn kernels and bell peppers, cubes of red potato and chunks of chicken. When corn is in season, it's worth the extra effort to make the chowder with fresh corn; at other seasons, use frozen corn kernels. There's no need to thaw frozen corn before adding it to the chowder.

1 In a large, heavy saucepan, combine the water, broth, chicken, potatoes, onions, bell peppers, celery, thyme, black pepper and salt; cover and bring to a boil over high heat. Reduce the heat to medium-low, cover and simmer, stirring occasionally, for 5 minutes.

2 Stir in the corn, cover and simmer, stirring occasionally, for 7 to 9 minutes, or until the corn and potatoes are tender.

3 Whisk the cornstarch into the milk, then stir the mixture into the soup. Increase the heat to medium-high and bring to a boil, stirring constantly. Simmer, stirring occasionally, for 2 to 3 minutes, or until the soup is thickened.

4 Stir the hot-pepper sauce into the soup and remove from the heat; cool the soup for 5 minutes, then whisk in the sour cream. Ladle the soup into bowls and garnish with chives, if desired.

Preparation time 15 minutes • **Total time** 35 minutes • **Per serving** 251 calories, 3.8 g. fat (14% of calories), 1.3 g. saturated fat, 39 mg. cholesterol, 414 mg. sodium, 4.2 g. dietary fiber, 87 mg. calcium, 2 mg. iron, 57 mg. vitamin C, 0.7 mg. beta-carotene • **Serves 4**

Cut off the pointed tip so that the cob is steady when you stand it on end.

Using a sharp knife, cut downward to slice the kernels from the cob.

LEMONY CHICKEN GUMBO WITH CHARD

1 pound skinless bone-in chicken
thighs

3½ cups water

1 cup defatted chicken broth

1 medium onion, diced

2 large carrots, sliced

¾ cup uncooked converted white
rice

2 garlic cloves, minced

¾ teaspoon dried mint, crumbled

½ teaspoon freshly ground black
pepper

⅛ teaspoon salt

4 cups firmly packed cut-up Swiss
chard or spinach (1-inch pieces)

1½ teaspoons grated lemon zest

1 tablespoon plus 1 teaspoon fresh
lemon juice

For a change, make the soup with red-stemmed chard, which looks almost like rhubarb.

The flavors of this soup are similar to those of the chicken, lemon and rice soup known in Greece as *avgolemono*. The Greek version, however, is thickened with eggs, while the broth here is unthickened and the soup is, instead, made more substantial with the addition of carrots and greens.

1 In a Dutch oven or large, heavy saucepan, combine the chicken thighs, water, broth, onions, carrots, rice, garlic, mint, pepper and salt; cover and bring to a boil over high heat. Reduce the heat to medium-low and simmer, stirring occasionally, for 10 to 15 minutes, or until the chicken is cooked through (the rice will not be done yet).

2 Using tongs, transfer the chicken thighs to a plate (scrape off any rice clinging to the chicken thighs and return it to the pot). Continue cooking the rice for 5 to 10 minutes longer, or until tender.

3 Meanwhile, place the chicken in the freezer for 5 to 10 minutes, or until cool enough to handle. Cut or pull the meat from the bones and tear into thin strips. Cover loosely with wax paper and set aside.

4 Stir the Swiss chard or spinach into the gumbo. Cover and cook, stirring once or twice, for 6 to 7 minutes, or until tender (spinach will require a minute or so less cooking time than chard). Add the chicken strips and stir until heated through.

5 Remove the pan from the heat and stir in the lemon zest and lemon juice. Ladle the soup into bowls and serve.

Preparation time 10 minutes • **Total time** 45 minutes • **Per serving** 285 calories, 4 g. fat (13% of calories), 0.9 g. saturated fat, 68 mg. cholesterol, 522 mg. sodium, 3 g. dietary fiber, 87 mg. calcium, 4 mg. iron, 30 mg. vitamin C, 10 mg. beta-carotene • **Serves 4**

❧ ❧ ❧

MAKE AHEAD

Complete the recipe through step 3 in advance; refrigerate the soup and chicken separately. Reheat over medium-low heat and continue with the recipe, adding the greens, chicken and lemon zest and juice.

NUTRITION NOTE

Thanks to the Swiss chard and lemon, a bowl of this soup provides about half of your daily requirement of vitamin C. The chard actually supplies more vitamin C than the lemon juice and lemon zest.

The Salad Bowl

❧ ❧ ❧

COOL, CASUAL MAIN DISHES

COMBINING POULTRY WITH

VEGETABLES AND FRUITS, POTATOES,

RICE OR PASTA

TROPICAL CHICKEN SALAD

2 tablespoons sliced natural
almonds

2 teaspoons ground cumin

1 cup defatted chicken broth

12 ounces skinless, boneless
chicken breast halves, cut into
1-inch chunks

1 tablespoon cornstarch dissolved
in 1 tablespoon cold water

¼ cup apricot nectar

1 tablespoon fresh lime juice

1 tablespoon honey

¼ teaspoon freshly ground
black pepper

⅛ teaspoon crushed red pepper
flakes

2 tablespoons chopped fresh
cilantro

2 cups fresh pineapple chunks
(or juice-packed canned
pineapple, drained)

Half of a ripe papaya, peeled,
seeded and cut into chunks
(1 cup)

1 ripe mango, peeled and cut into
chunks (1 cup)

4 cups (1 large bunch) watercress
or spinach, washed and trimmed

Pineapples, with their natural "armor," have been shipped to this country since the eighteenth century, but thinner-skinned mangoes and papayas are not such good travelers. Fortunately, they're now grown in Hawaii, Florida and California, and are available in most supermarkets. When ripe, mangoes and papayas will yield to gentle pressure; if necessary, ripen them in paper bags for a few days.

1 In a heavy, medium no-stick skillet, toast the almonds over medium-high heat, tossing frequently, for about 4 minutes, or until lightly browned. Tip the almonds onto a plate to stop the cooking.

2 Add the cumin to the skillet and cook over medium heat, stirring frequently, for about 4 minutes, or until the cumin is toasted and fragrant. Immediately transfer half of the cumin to a salad bowl; pour the broth into the skillet and bring to a boil over high heat.

3 Add the chicken to the skillet and reduce the heat to medium; cover and cook, stirring frequently, for 3 to 4 minutes, or until the chicken is cooked through. With a slotted spoon, transfer the chicken to a plate; cover it with wax paper to keep it moist.

4 Increase the heat to high and bring the cooking liquid to a boil. Boil for about 3 minutes, or until the liquid is reduced to about ¼ cup. Stir in the cornstarch mixture and return to a boil, whisking constantly (the mixture will be extremely thick). Remove from the heat.

5 Scrape the thickened liquid into the salad bowl and whisk in the apricot nectar, lime juice, honey, black pepper and red pepper; continue whisking until smooth. Stir in the cilantro.

6 Add to the bowl the chicken and any juices that have collected on the plate, the pineapple, papaya and mango, and toss gently to mix.

7 Spread the watercress or spinach on a large platter. Top with the chicken salad and sprinkle with the toasted almonds.

Preparation time 25 minutes • **Total time** 35 minutes • **Per serving** 238 calories, 3.7 g. fat (14% of calories), 0.5 g. saturated fat, 49 mg. cholesterol, 322 mg. sodium, 2.7 g. dietary fiber, 90 mg. calcium, 2 mg. iron, 71 mg. vitamin C, 3 mg. beta-carotene
Serves 4

❧   ❧   ❧

Preceding pages: Fruited Chicken and
Couscous Salad (recipe on page 107)

CHICKEN SALAD NIÇOISE

1 **pound small red potatoes, cut into 1-inch wedges**

1 **cup defatted chicken broth**

½ **cup water**

2 **garlic cloves, peeled**

½ **teaspoon freshly ground black pepper**

¼ **teaspoon dried thyme**

12 **ounces skinless, boneless chicken breast halves, cut crosswise into l-inch strips**

8 **ounces green beans**

1 **tablespoon plus 1 teaspoon extra-virgin olive oil**

1 **tablespoon plus 2 teaspoons white wine vinegar**

1 **teaspoon Dijon mustard**

⅛ **teaspoon salt**

4 **ripe plum tomatoes, cut into wedges**

1 **medium kirby cucumber, halved crosswise and cut into wedges**

8 **kalamata olives**

⅓ **cup julienne-cut basil leaves**

You've probably eaten a bountiful *salade Niçoise* made with canned tuna, and perhaps you've also enjoyed a modern version with fresh tuna. The same vegetables and dressing that set off the fish so beautifully work equally well with poached chicken.

1 Place the potatoes in a medium saucepan and add cold water to cover; cover the pan and bring to a boil over high heat. Reduce the heat to medium and simmer for 10 to 12 minutes, or until the potatoes are fork-tender. Drain in a colander and set aside to cool slightly.

2 While the potatoes are cooking, in another medium saucepan, combine the broth, water, garlic cloves, ¼ teaspoon of the pepper and the thyme; bring to a boil over high heat. Reduce the heat to medium, stir in the chicken strips and simmer, stirring frequently, for 3 to 4 minutes, or until the chicken is cooked through. Using a slotted spoon, transfer the chicken to a plate; cover loosely with wax paper and set aside. Remove and discard the garlic cloves.

3 Add the green beans to the poaching liquid, increase the heat to high and bring to a boil. Simmer, stirring occasionally, for 5 to 6 minutes, or until the beans are crisp-tender. Using a slotted spoon, transfer the beans to a small strainer and rinse briefly under cold running water to stop the cooking.

4 Measure out and discard ½ cup of the poaching liquid. Increase the heat under the saucepan to high and bring to a boil. Boil for about 3 minutes, or until the liquid is reduced to about 2 tablespoons. Transfer the reduced liquid to a large bowl. Whisk in the oil, vinegar, mustard, salt and the remaining ¼ teaspoon pepper. Add the cooked potatoes, chicken and green beans, and toss to coat well.

5 Transfer the chicken, potatoes and green beans to a shallow serving bowl. Add the tomato and cucumber wedges and the olives, and sprinkle the salad with the basil.

Preparation time 20 minutes • **Total time** 45 minutes • **Per serving** 289 calories, 7.5 g. fat (23% of calories), 1.1 g. saturated fat, 49 mg. cholesterol, 379 mg. sodium, 4.9 g. dietary fiber, 78 mg. calcium, 4 mg. iron, 52 mg. vitamin C, 0.8 mg. beta-carotene • **Serves 4**

❧ ❧ ❧

CHICKEN AND RADIATORE SALAD

8 ounces radiatore pasta

12 ounces fresh asparagus spears, trimmed and cut diagonally into 1-inch lengths

3 medium carrots, thinly sliced

½ cup defatted chicken broth

½ cup water

3 tablespoons fresh lemon juice

2 garlic cloves, halved

¾ teaspoon dried tarragon

12 ounces skinless, boneless chicken breast halves, cut into ¾-inch chunks

2 cups loosely packed spinach leaves, well washed

¾ cup cut-up scallions

½ cup packed Italian parsley sprigs

¼ cup reduced-calorie mayonnaise

1 teaspoon Dijon mustard

¾ teaspoon freshly ground black pepper

¼ teaspoon salt

1 medium kirby cucumber, thinly sliced

Many of America's favorite salads and dressings originated in California, including a blend of mayonnaise, tarragon vinegar, garlic and fresh herbs created in San Francisco in the 1920s and dubbed "Green Goddess dressing." That's the inspiration for the herb dressing here; it's tossed with mouth-filling radiatore pasta, crisp-tender asparagus and chunks of poached chicken.

1 Bring a large covered pot of water to a boil over high heat. Add the radiatore and return to a boil. Cook for 7 minutes, then stir in the asparagus and carrots and cook for 1 to 2 minutes longer, or until the vegetables are crisp-tender and the pasta is al dente. Drain in a colander, rinse briefly under cold running water and drain again.

2 Meanwhile, combine the broth, water, 1 teaspoon of the lemon juice, the garlic cloves and tarragon in a medium skillet; cover and bring to a boil over high heat. Add the chicken and reduce the heat to medium; cover and simmer, stirring frequently, for 4 to 5 minutes, or until the chicken is just cooked through. Using a slotted spoon, transfer the chicken to a bowl; cover loosely with a sheet of wax paper to keep moist.

3 Stir the spinach, scallions and parsley into the broth mixture and place over high heat. Cook, stirring frequently, for 1 to 2 minutes, or until the greens are just wilted. Drain the greens and garlic cloves through a large strainer set over a bowl; reserve 3 tablespoons of the cooking liquid and discard the remainder.

4 Combine the greens, garlic and reserved cooking liquid in a food processor, and process until puréed. Add the mayonnaise, mustard, pepper, salt and the remaining 2 tablespoons plus 2 teaspoons lemon juice, and process just until blended.

5 Combine the pasta mixture, chicken and cucumbers in a salad bowl. Add the dressing and toss to mix.

Preparation time 20 minutes • **Total time** 40 minutes • **Per serving** 406 calories, 6.6 g. fat (15% of calories), 1.5 g. saturated fat, 54 mg. cholesterol, 430 mg. sodium, 5.7 g. dietary fiber, 116 mg. calcium, 6 mg. iron, 50 mg. vitamin C, 11 mg. beta-carotene • **Serves 4**

Chinese Chicken and Noodle Salad

1 cup defatted chicken broth

3 tablespoons rice vinegar

1 slice (¼ inch thick) fresh ginger plus 1 tablespoon grated ginger

12 ounces skinless, boneless chicken breast halves

8 ounces vermicelli pasta

2 tablespoons reduced-sodium soy sauce

1 garlic clove, crushed through a press

2 teaspoons dark sesame oil

1 teaspoon granulated sugar

¼ teaspoon crushed red pepper flakes

3 cups shredded napa cabbage

1 cup julienne-cut snow peas

½ cup shredded carrots

½ cup minced fresh cilantro

When crinkly napa cabbage is cut crosswise, it falls naturally into strips that separate easily.

There are macaroni salads made with mayonnaise and pasta salads made with pesto, but the Chinese pairing of noodles and sesame sauce is in a class by itself. This version is lower in fat than the traditional Szechuan noodles dish.

1 Bring a large covered pot of water to a boil over high heat.

2 In a medium skillet, combine the broth, 1 tablespoon of the vinegar and the ginger slice; cover and bring to a boil over high heat.

3 Add the chicken breasts to the skillet; reduce the heat to medium-low (the liquid should be barely simmering). Cover and simmer, turning the chicken two or three times, for 8 to 10 minutes, or until cooked through. Transfer the chicken to a plate; cover loosely with a sheet of wax paper and let stand until cool enough to handle. Remove the ginger from the poaching liquid and reserve ½ cup of the liquid.

4 While the chicken cools, add the pasta to the boiling water; return to a boil and cook for 6 to 8 minutes, or according to package directions until al dente. Drain in a colander, rinse briefly under cold running water and drain again. Transfer the pasta to a salad bowl and toss with ¼ cup of the reserved poaching liquid.

5 In a small bowl, whisk the remaining ¼ cup poaching liquid with the remaining 2 tablespoons vinegar, the grated ginger, soy sauce, garlic, sesame oil, sugar and red pepper flakes.

6 Cut the chicken into fine shreds. Add the chicken to the pasta, then add the cabbage, snow peas, carrots and cilantro. Pour the dressing over the salad and toss to coat.

Preparation time 15 minutes • **Total time** 40 minutes • **Per serving** 371 calories, 4.6 g. fat (11% of calories), 0.8 g. saturated fat, 49 mg. cholesterol, 496 mg. sodium, 3.3 g. dietary fiber, 89 mg. calcium, 4 mg. iron, 40 mg. vitamin C, 3 mg. beta-carotene
Serves 4

ON THE MENU
Cups of hot tea or glasses of iced tea are just the thing to serve with this Chinese-style salad. For dessert, offer a platter of navel oranges and thin almond cookies or vanilla wafers.

TURKEY AND SWEET POTATO SALAD

- ¾ **cup nonfat yogurt**
- 1 **pound sweet potatoes, peeled and cut into 1-inch chunks**
- ½ **cup defatted chicken broth**
- ¼ **cup water**
- 3 **tablespoons frozen orange juice concentrate, thawed**
- 2 **teaspoons curry powder**
- 12 **ounces skinless, boneless turkey breast, cut into ½-inch cubes**
- 2 **celery stalks, diagonally sliced**
- 3 **scallions, diagonally sliced**
- 3 **tablespoons raisins**
- ¼ **cup mango chutney**
- ⅛ **teaspoon hot-pepper sauce**
- ⅛ **teaspoon salt**
- 3 **tablespoons coarsely chopped toasted pecans**

When Thanksgiving is a distant memory, cook some fresh turkey and sweet potatoes for this delectable warm salad, tossed with an orange-curry-chutney dressing that's like nothing you've ever eaten on "Turkey Day."

1 Line a small strainer with cheesecloth or paper towels and suspend it over a small bowl. Spoon the yogurt into the strainer and let drain for 15 minutes. Discard the whey and dry the bowl; turn the drained yogurt into the bowl.

2 While the yogurt is draining, place the sweet potatoes in a medium saucepan and add cold water to cover. Cover and bring to a boil over high heat. Reduce the heat to medium and simmer for 9 to 11 minutes, or until the sweet potatoes are fork-tender but not mushy. Drain in a colander and cool briefly under gently running cold water.

3 In a medium skillet, combine the broth, water, 1 tablespoon of the orange juice concentrate and 1 teaspoon of the curry powder; cover and bring to a boil over high heat.

4 Stir the turkey cubes into the broth mixture, reduce the heat to medium, cover and cook, stirring frequently, for 4 to 5 minutes, or until the turkey is cooked through. Reserving 3 tablespoons of the cooking liquid, drain the turkey in a colander.

5 Place the sweet potatoes in a large salad bowl and add the turkey, celery, scallions and raisins.

6 To the yogurt, add the reserved turkey cooking liquid, the remaining 2 tablespoons orange juice concentrate, remaining 1 teaspoon curry powder, the chutney, hot-pepper sauce and salt, and stir to blend.

7 Pour the dressing over the salad and toss gently to coat. Sprinkle with the pecans and serve.

Preparation time 20 minutes • **Total time** 40 minutes • **Per serving** 342 calories, 4.7 g. fat (12% of calories), 0.6 g. saturated fat, 54 mg. cholesterol, 479 mg. sodium, 4.2 g. dietary fiber, 143 mg. calcium, 2 mg. iron, 41 mg. vitamin C, 9.9 mg. beta-carotene • **Serves 4**

COBB SALAD WITH PARMESAN DRESSING

½ cup low-fat buttermilk

3 tablespoons grated Parmesan cheese

2 tablespoons light sour cream

1 tablespoon distilled white vinegar

¾ teaspoon coarsely cracked black pepper

⅛ teaspoon salt

3 cups loosely packed torn red-leaf lettuce

1 medium head Boston lettuce, torn into bite-size pieces (about 3 cups)

1 can (16 ounces) chick-peas, rinsed and drained

4 ounces julienne-cut skinless roast turkey breast

Whites of 4 hard-cooked eggs, coarsely chopped

Half of a ripe medium avocado, cut into chunks

1½ cups halved cherry tomatoes

½ cup thinly sliced radishes

A California classic, the Cobb salad was a signature dish of the Brown Derby restaurant in Hollywood. It's a sort of salad-bar-in-a-dish, with finely chopped greens, herbs, chicken, eggs, bacon, tomatoes and blue cheese arrayed in broad bands in a big bowl. The salad is first displayed in all its multicolored glory, then tossed with a vinaigrette. Here, the components are cut into more substantial pieces and arranged on a platter; toss the salad gently before serving, or simply pour on the dressing and pass the platter around.

1 To make the dressing, in a small bowl, whisk together the buttermilk, Parmesan, sour cream, vinegar, pepper and salt.

2 Spread the red-leaf and Boston lettuces in a large, shallow bowl or on a platter. Arrange the chick-peas, turkey, egg whites, avocados, cherry tomatoes and radishes in even bands over the lettuce.

3 Drizzle the dressing over the salad, toss if desired and serve.

Preparation time 30 minutes • **Total time** 30 minutes • **Per serving** 243 calories, 8.7 g. fat (32% of calories), 2.2 g. saturated fat, 30 mg. cholesterol, 384 mg. sodium, 5.3 g. dietary fiber, 188 mg. calcium, 4 mg. iron, 30 mg. vitamin C, 1 mg. beta-carotene • **Serves 4**

Halve the avocado, then tap the blade of a heavy knife against the pit; use the knife like a screwdriver to twist out the pit.

Grasp the skin at the blossom end and pull. The skin should come off smoothly, leaving the flesh unmarked.

DILLED CHICKEN AND POTATO SALAD

1 cup defatted chicken broth

½ cup water

3 tablespoons cider vinegar

¾ teaspoon freshly ground
   black pepper

¼ teaspoon dill seeds

1¼ pounds small red potatoes, cut
   into 1-inch chunks

⅓ cup nonfat yogurt

8 ounces skinless, boneless
   chicken breast halves, cut into
   ¾-inch cubes

3 tablespoons reduced-calorie
   mayonnaise

2 tablespoons snipped fresh dill

1 large red bell pepper, coarsely
   diced

1 large ripe tomato, diced

⅓ cup sliced scallions

Cooking the potatoes in well-seasoned broth gives you a head start on a full-flavored potato salad. After the potatoes are done, the chicken is poached in the same broth. The warm potatoes and chicken are combined, while still warm, in a tart yogurt dressing, and the salad is best if served immediately. Instead of fresh dill, you might try parsley, thyme, tarragon or another favorite herb.

1 In a medium saucepan, combine the broth, water, 2 tablespoons of the vinegar, ½ teaspoon of the black pepper and the dill seeds. Cover and bring to a boil over high heat.

2 Add the potatoes to the broth mixture and return to a boil. Reduce the heat to medium, cover and simmer for 10 to 15 minutes, or until the potatoes are fork-tender. Using a slotted spoon, transfer the potatoes to a salad bowl.

3 While the potatoes are cooking, line a small strainer with cheesecloth or paper towels and suspend it over a small bowl. Spoon the yogurt into the strainer and let drain for 15 minutes. Discard the whey and dry the bowl. Turn the yogurt into the bowl.

4 Add the chicken cubes to the broth mixture, cover and simmer, stirring frequently, for 2 to 4 minutes, or until the chicken is cooked through. Drain the chicken in a colander, then add it to the potatoes. Set aside the chicken and potatoes to cool slightly.

5 To the yogurt, add the mayonnaise, fresh dill, remaining 1 tablespoon vinegar and remaining ¼ teaspoon black pepper, and whisk until blended. Pour the dressing over the chicken and potatoes. Add the bell peppers, tomatoes and scallions, and toss to mix.

Preparation time 30 minutes • **Total time** 30 minutes • **Per serving** 246 calories, 4.6 g. fat (17% of calories), 1 g. saturated fat, 37 mg. cholesterol, 376 mg. sodium, 3.5 g. dietary fiber, 67 mg. calcium, 2 mg. iron, 79 mg. vitamin C, 1 mg. beta-carotene
Serves 4

FOODWAYS
Potato salad is popular in many parts of the world. The Germans make theirs with bacon; the French toss hot potatoes with white wine. Scandinavians mix diced potatoes with chopped apples and beets.

FRUITED CHICKEN AND COUSCOUS SALAD

½ cup defatted chicken broth

⅔ cup water

¾ cup instant couscous

¼ cup slivered dried apricots

2 tablespoons golden raisins

2 medium navel oranges

2 tablespoons fresh lemon juice

2 tablespoons chopped red onion

1 tablespoon extra-virgin olive oil

1 tablespoon honey

½ teaspoon freshly ground black pepper

¼ teaspoon salt

⅛ teaspoon ground red pepper

12 ounces skinless, boneless chicken breast halves, cut crosswise into ½-inch-wide strips

½ teaspoon ground coriander

1 large red bell pepper, cut into thin strips

½ cup thinly sliced fennel or celery

4 cups colorful mixed greens, torn into bite-size pieces

Couscous is a granular pasta made from semolina flour and water. Delicately flavored, it readily absorbs savory or sweet sauces, gravies and dressings. In Morocco, couscous is steamed slowly over a pot of spicy stew, but the instant couscous you'll find in your supermarket just needs to steep briefly in boiling liquid.

1 In a medium saucepan, bring the broth and water to a boil over high heat. Stir in the couscous, apricots and raisins, and remove the pan from the heat. Cover and let stand for 5 minutes, or until the couscous has absorbed the liquid. Spread the couscous in a shallow baking dish and place in the freezer for 10 minutes to chill.

2 Preheat the broiler. Spray a jelly-roll pan with no-stick spray.

3 Using a scrrated knife, pare the peel and pith from the oranges. Working over a medium bowl, cut out the sections from between the membranes; set the sections aside. Squeeze the juice from the membranes into a large bowl: You should have about 3 tablespoons of juice.

4 To the orange juice, add 1 tablespoon of the lemon juice, the red onions, oil, honey, ¼ teaspoon of the black pepper, ⅛ teaspoon of the salt and half of the ground red pepper.

5 Place the chicken strips in the prepared pan and sprinkle with the coriander, the remaining 1 tablespoon lemon juice, remaining ¼ teaspoon black pepper, remaining ⅛ teaspoon salt and remaining ground red pepper. Toss the chicken to season evenly.

6 Broil the chicken 4 to 5 inches from the heat, turning the pieces several times, for 4 to 6 minutes, or until cooked through.

7 Add the chilled couscous, the chicken, bell peppers and fennel or celery to the dressing, and toss to mix. Add the orange sections and toss gently. Spread the greens on a platter and mound the couscous mixture in the center.

Preparation time 20 minutes • **Total time** 30 minutes • **Per serving** 363 calories, 5.5 g. fat (14% of calories), 0.3 g. saturated fat, 49 mg. cholesterol, 339 mg. sodium, 4 g. dietary fiber, 95 mg. calcium, 3 mg. iron, 106 mg. vitamin C, 2 mg. beta-carotene
Serves 4

Thai Rice and Turkey Salad

1 cup uncooked converted white rice

2½ cups water

½ cup defatted chicken broth

1 tablespoon grated fresh ginger

2 garlic cloves, crushed through a press

12 ounces skinless, boneless turkey breast, cut crosswise into strips

3 tablespoons no-salt-added peanut butter

3 tablespoons fresh lime juice

1 teaspoon honey

½ teaspoon anchovy paste

¼ teaspoon salt

¼ teaspoon crushed red pepper flakes

2 cups shredded napa cabbage

1 large red bell pepper, diced

½ cup diced red onion

3 tablespoons coarsely chopped fresh mint

3 cups small tender kale leaves or spinach, well washed

2 tablespoons coarsely chopped roasted unsalted peanuts

Balance is the keynote of Thai meals, and menus are carefully planned to touch on five flavors: sweet, hot, sour, salty and even a touch of bitter. A root called *galanga,* citrusy lemongrass and *nam pla,* a pungent fish sauce, are Thai staples. Here, ginger, lime juice and anchovy paste stand in for these exotic ingredients.

1 In a heavy medium saucepan, combine the rice and 2 cups of the water, and bring to a boil over high heat. Reduce the heat to low, cover and simmer for 20 minutes, or until the rice is tender and the liquid is absorbed. Spread the rice in a shallow baking pan and place it in the freezer for about 10 minutes to chill slightly.

2 Meanwhile, in a medium skillet, combine the remaining ½ cup water with the broth, ginger and garlic; cover and bring to a boil over high heat. Reduce the heat to medium and simmer for 5 minutes to blend the flavors. Stir in the turkey strips, cover and cook, stirring frequently, for 3 to 4 minutes, or until the turkey is cooked through.

3 Using a slotted spoon, transfer the turkey to a plate; cover loosely with a sheet of wax paper to keep it moist.

4 Increase the heat under the skillet to high and return the broth to a boil. Boil rapidly for 5 to 6 minutes, or until the broth is thickened and reduced to about ¼ cup.

5 In a salad bowl, whisk together the peanut butter, lime juice, honey, anchovy paste, salt and red pepper flakes. Whisk in the reduced broth and continue whisking until smooth (whisk in a few drops of hot water if the mixture becomes too thick). Add the cooled rice, the turkey strips and any juices that have collected on the plate, and stir gently; then add the cabbage, bell peppers, onions and mint, and toss to mix.

6 Arrange the kale or spinach leaves on a platter. Mound the salad in the center and sprinkle with the peanuts.

Preparation time 20 minutes • **Total time** 45 minutes • **Per serving** 432 calories, 10.2 g. fat (21% of calories), 1 g. saturated fat, 53 mg. cholesterol, 359 mg. sodium, 5.7 g. dietary fiber, 154 mg. calcium, 4 mg. iron, 126 mg. vitamin C, 3.9 mg. beta-carotene • **Serves 4**

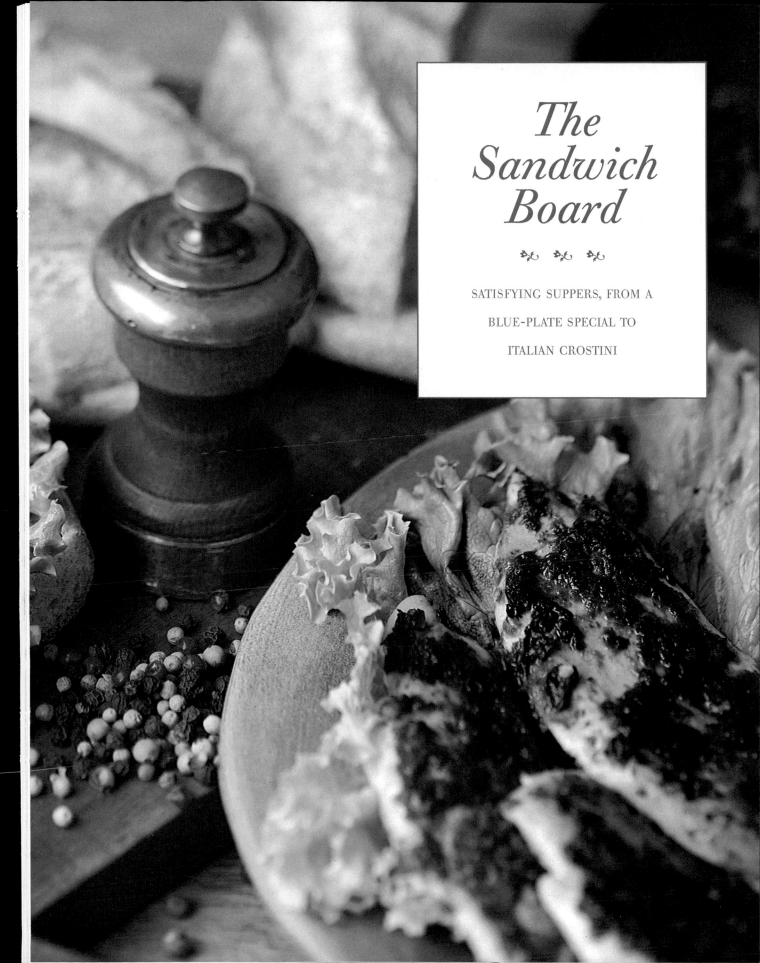

The Sandwich Board

❧ ❧ ❧

SATISFYING SUPPERS, FROM A

BLUE-PLATE SPECIAL TO

ITALIAN CROSTINI

TURKEY AND SWISS WITH SLAW

3 tablespoons nonfat yogurt

1 tablespoon plus 1 teaspoon chili sauce

1 tablespoon reduced-calorie mayonnaise

1 tablespoon minced red onion or scallion

2 teaspoons red wine vinegar

1 teaspoon prepared white horseradish

¼ teaspoon freshly ground black pepper

2 cups finely shredded red cabbage

½ cup shredded carrots

6 ounces sliced skinless roast turkey breast

8 slices rye bread

2 ounces sliced Swiss cheese

Not too far back in the ancestry of this hearty meal is the famous Reuben sandwich, named for the New York City deli owner who created it. The original Reuben packed a hefty payload between two slices of rye bread: Russian dressing, corned beef, Swiss cheese and sauerkraut, in generous portions. Although these "light Reubens" are considerably trimmed down by using turkey, homemade slaw and a single slice of cheese, they are still somewhat high in sodium. Most of the sodium comes from the bread, and much smaller quantities from the chili sauce and cheese.

1 In a medium bowl, stir together the yogurt, chili sauce, mayonnaise, onions or scallions, vinegar, horseradish and pepper.

2 Add the cabbage and carrots to the yogurt mixture, and toss until the vegetables are well coated.

3 Divide the turkey among 4 slices of the bread. Spoon some slaw over the turkey, then top with cheese and a second slice of bread.

Preparation time 20 minutes • **Total time** 20 minutes • **Per serving** 316 calories, 7.5 g. fat (21% of calories), 3.3 g. saturated fat, 50 mg. cholesterol, 596 mg. sodium, 5.2 g. dietary fiber, 234 mg. calcium, 3 mg. iron, 23 mg. vitamin C, 2 mg. beta-carotene • **Serves 4**

SUBSTITUTIONS

If you need to watch your sodium intake, use lower-sodium versions of the bread, chili sauce and cheese. The sodium content of bread varies widely: This recipe was analyzed with rye bread containing 211 mg. of sodium per slice, but by reading the nutrition labels on bread packages you may well find a brand with less. Low-sodium ketchup can stand in for the chili sauce, and reduced-sodium Swiss cheese is sold in many supermarkets.

HEAD START

Make the cabbage-and-carrot slaw in advance and refrigerate it.

KITCHEN TIPS

To make shredding the carrots easier, spray the grater with no-stick spray.

FOR A CHANGE

Broil the sandwiches open-face until the cheese melts, then top with the second slice of bread.

INDEX

❧ ❧ ❧